THE STONE SPEAKS

The Memoir of a Personal Transformation

Maud Oakes

Foreword by William McGuire
Introduction by Joseph L. Henderson

Chiron Publications

Wilmette, Illinois

THE STONE SPEAKS

The Memoir of a Personal Transformation

Maud Oakes

C. G. Jung

Printed in the United States of America

Edited by Carole Presser
Book design by Kirk G. Panikis

Grateful acknowledgment is made to the following:
Allen & Unwin for permission to quote from *The Way and Its Power*, by Arthur Waley.
Estate of C. G. Jung for permission to reprint the letters of Jan. 31, 1956, Feb. 2, 1956, and Oct. 3, 1957, between Dr. Jung and Miss Oakes.
Harcourt Brace Jovanovich for permission to reprint excerpts from "Four Quartets" in *The Collected Poems of T. S. Eliot, 1909–62*, and from *The Way of Individuation*, by Jolande Jacobi.
J. G. Ferguson Publishing Company for permission to quote from *Man and His Symbols*, by Carl G. Jung et al. copyright 1964.
Pantheon Books for permission to quote from *Memories, Dreams, Reflections*, by C. G. Jung, recorded and edited by Aniela Jaffé, trans. Richard and Clara Winston.
Princeton University Press for permission to quote *in passim* from *The Collected Works of C. G. Jung*, trans. R. F. C. Hull, Bollingen Series XX.

Library of Congress Cataloging-in-Publication Data

Oakes, Maud, 1903–
   The stone speaks.

   Bibliography: p.
   1. Jung, C. G. (Carl Gustav), 1875–1961—Correspondence. 2. Oakes, Maud, 1903–   —Correspondence. 3. Psychoanalysts—Switzerland. 4. Anthropologist—United States. I. Title.
BF173.J85O24   1987   150.19′54   86-23252
ISBN 0-933029-23-3
ISBN 0-933029-04-7 pbk.

Contents

Jung's Stone in Winter

Detail of Jung's Stone

Foreword

The journey of Maud Van Cortlandt Oakes from an island in Puget Sound to the edge of Lake Zürich and beyond followed a singular itinerary, whether interior or exterior. Her book gives the stunning particulars of the inner way, though it affords only glimpses of certain of the outer stations of her long life. A more explicit account cannot rob her story of its extraordinary quality.

Born in Seattle in 1903, Maud grew up on one of the numerous islands that dot the Sound. As a girl she discovered troves of American Indian artifacts and became aware of the lore and art of the Northwest Coast tribes. A literary immersion in the novels of Fenimore Cooper fixed her impressions. Her family was allied to pioneer traditions, not the least of which were the great intercontinental railroads. She went east to study at the Art Students League in New York, modestly aiming at a career in commercial art. Unsatisfied, she went to Europe, traveled, made lighthearted movies with her cousin Jerome Hill and his Yale classmate John Barrett, and settled in at Fontainebleau for more serious art studies. There, G. I. Gurdjieff's Institute for the Harmonious Development of Man faintly struck a responsive chord, though too faintly to make her a disciple. More to her inner purpose was the great ethnological museum in the Palais du Trocadéro, in Paris, where her feeling for primitive art and culture was nourished, and she became aware of symbolism. A personal collection of books and art began to take form.

In New York in the 1930s, through Jack Barrett, she came to know the friends who were to have much to do with the shaping of her later life—Nancy Wilson Ross, another Northwesterner, who was curiously exploring philosophies, systems, and religions, and beginning her career as a novelist and student of the Orient; the art dealer Marian Willard; and Mary Conover, who also belonged to the business world of art and was another seeker. Nancy Ross persuaded Maud to try analysis with a therapist who followed some of Jung's teachings (in those years, "official" accreditation did not exist in the world of Jungian psychology); as Maud tells it, the experience was not a success. Mary Conover meanwhile had married Paul Mellon, and both had begun Jungian analysis. In 1937, the Mellons took Maud with them to meetings of Jung's seminar on "Dream Symbols of the Individuation Process" in a New York club. After the first meeting, Maud dreamed of finding a red rose blooming in a castle moat. She began to read Jung, and her paintings now expressed the symbolic. Mary and Paul Mellon meanwhile had gone to Zürich to work analytically with Jung and Toni Wolff, and had met Olga Froebe-Kapteyn, the sibylline leader of the Eranos Conferences at Ascona.

At the outbreak of the war in Europe, when they had to return to the United States, Mary Mellon was determined to publish Jung's works and books of related interest. In her planning of what she named the Bollingen Foundation—in honor of the secluded country retreat that Jung, an amateur stonemason, had built on the edge of Lake Zürich, well away from the city—she enlisted the help of the Indologist Heinrich Zimmer, who had fled from Nazi Germany and brought his family to settle in New York. When, in 1941, Olga Froebe-Kapteyn came to the United States to research archetypal pictures for her Eranos Archive, a remark of hers—"You Americans don't know your own heritage. You know nothing about the American Indian!"—fired Maud Oakes with the determination to work with the Navaho shamans, whose sandpaintings she had read about in an anthropological study. With a small monthly stipend from Paul Mellon (anticipating the fellowships awarded by the Bollingen Foundation, which had not yet been formally established), she spent two years in New Mexico near the Navaho reservation. Quite on her own, Maud pursued the studies with medicine men and created the paintings that, encouraged by Zimmer, resulted in the first book in Mary Mellon's Bollingen Series: *Where the Two Came to Their Father*. The publication, commended by scholars, comprised

Maud's recording of the Blessing Ceremony for young warriors, her careful and beautiful copies of the sandpaintings used in the ritual, and a mythological commentary by a young protégé of Zimmer's, Joseph Campbell.

From Zimmer, Maud learned the symbolism of the Tarot cards and their use in divination. His sudden death in 1943 was a dreadful loss to the Bollingen program. Maud found still other teachers in the circle that had formed around Mary Mellon and Bollingen. One was Natacha Rambova, an American student of mythology, symbolism, theosophy, and kindred lore, whose classes in her New York apartment Maud attended. Maud's stipend for her Navaho project had been the beginning of the Bollingen fellowships, and the earliest group of Bollingen fellows numbered also Rambova and Paul Radin, revered anthropologist of the American Indian, from whose insights and disciplines Maud learned richly.

Inspired by both Radin and Rambova, Maud embarked on another solitary project—it was still wartime, in 1944—in a remote mountain village in Guatemala, where she spent nearly two years. Rambova visited and encouraged her. Maud Oakes's unique study of Mayan religious survivals among the superficially Christian Indians, *The Two Crosses of Todos Santos* (Bollingen Series, 1951), was the achievement. In October 1946, while Maud was in Todos Santos, Mary Mellon's quite unexpected death threatened to end the Bollingen enterprise. Her last words to her husband—"I had so much to do!"—heartened him to carry the Foundation on, under the leadership of John Barrett.

The following year, after completing her fieldwork, Maud spent a winter in Egypt, where Rambova had gone to study symbolism. While working on *The Two Crosses*, Maud also became interested in Egyptian esoterica. After observing Rambova's work in the Valley of the Kings, Maud urged the Bollingen Foundation to support Rambova's plan for a systematic recording of the representations in the most important tombs. Rambova, in collaboration with an eminent Egyptologist, Alexandre Piankoff, organized an expedition under Bollingen auspices that produced materials yielding six volumes on Egyptian Religious Texts and Representations.

Big Sur was Maud's next way station. She bought a house high on the cliffs, overlooking the Pacific Ocean, where seasonal schools of whales were clearly visible. Her nearest neighbor and friend was the writer Henry Miller. Another was the artist Louisa Jenkins. Maud devoted herself to writing, painting, and the study of myth and symbol, interrupting her work only for an interlude in New York to attend a class Rambova was teaching on astronomical symbolism in the Mysteries. In 1950 she began to plan a stay in India, to study the religion and art of a primitive people, the Nagas, but political unrest made her give up the project. She decided instead on Peru, to investigate the remains of Inca culture. That story, with its violent and disappointing outcome in the Andes, she tells in vivid detail, and how she went to France and then to Switzerland for convalescence, and discovered Jung's Stone, with its numinous inscriptions. It establishes the core of her present book.

After Maud returned to her eyrie at Big Sur, buried herself in Jung's writings, and decided to enter Jungian analysis, a new pattern began to appear in her life: a circling back, in the way that Jung himself dealt with his alchemical explorations. Intermittently she returned to her Navaho interest, lectured, executed sandpaintings, and contributed a recorded myth with the relevant paintings to L. C. Wyman's *Beautyway: A Navaho Ceremonial* (Bollingen, 1957). With Joseph Henderson she collaborated on a book about the symbolism of the Serpent. In 1954 she resumed her study of the Maya and planned to explore the deciphering of the Mayan glyphs. When her house at Big Sur burned down, along with her paintings, papers, and books, she read that as a signal. She rebuilt, set off on a trip around the world with her godchild, Cathy Mellon, and returned to the still center that Jung's Stone represented. Eventually, as life in remote Big Sur became problematical, she moved her home closer to San Francisco —to Mill Valley, then to Carmel—and played a concerned role in the work of the C. G. Jung Institute of San Francisco. The Institute made her an honorary member, for life, of its Board of Governors. The Bollingen Foundation, which she had joined in creating and nurturing, gradually completed its mission, leaving its thousand and one legacies.

As Maud Oakes traced and retraced the pages of her manuscript, it has become more than the story of a richly and mysteriously carved Stone—rather, it is the parable of her own inner life, her own search and discovery.

William McGuire

Introduction

Miss Oakes tells us that she first became acquainted with a stone sculpture carved by Professor C. G. Jung when she encountered it in his garden at Bollingen. Six months later, while recuperating from an illness, she placed a photograph of the stone before her as an object of meditation. In this respect she shows herself to be the type of anthropologist capable of using some of the wisdom she had gained from studying people of alien cultures, to meet her own personal needs. If a Navaho Indian is ill, he calls upon a medicine man to make a sandpainting for the occasion and to recite the appropriate chantway to cure the illness. Like the Navaho patient, Miss Oakes, who studied Navaho ceremonials and sandpaintings, understood the need for psychic as well as physical treatment. Accordingly, she adopted Jung as her symbolic medicine man for the psychic aspect of her treatment, and his stone as her sandpainting. Unlike the Navaho patient, she set herself the task of discovering its meaning by herself. Only later did she communicate her impressions to Jung, and ask his advice and comment.

The procession of events that occurs in such a psychic exercise has been described in this study as a series of three subjective states of being: *meditation, healing,* and *transformation.* My own experience as an analytical psychologist verifies this three-step progression in those patients who have spontaneously learned to experience the archetypes of the unconscious as part of a process of active imagination. The constancy of this pattern, as revealed in the content of such psychic products, is represented by three aspects or stages of development in an archetype of initiation.*

What is of special interest in Miss Oakes's account of her own experience is that she did not choose a Navaho sandpainting or a Tibetan mandala as an object for her meditation. She chose Jung's stone. She instinctively recognized a truth so often expressed by Jung in his writings: For Western man the religious products of alien cultures are usually unnatural. We do better to stick to the archetypal forms contained within our own spiritual traditions. The stone, with its inscriptions in Latin and Greek and its special symbolizations, place it firmly within the tradition of Greco-Roman religious and philosophic thought.

Exactly in the center of the inner circle is a figure that would have been familiar to the ancient Greeks of 500–600 B.C.: Telesphorus, the child-companion of Aesculapius, the god of healing, who is at the same time marked by the symbol ☿ for Hermes-Mercury. This points to a tradition concerned with the principle of psychic transformation, preserved as a secret form of initiation well into the Christian era. In the composite figure of Telesphorus and Hermes, it is as if Jung indirectly refers to his own work as a psychological doctor for whom *healing* became synonymous with *transformation*.

It is as if Jung, in his own very individual way of experiencing the ancient images, carved in the stone an indication that the cure for our modern sickness of mind comes from a much deeper level than could be found in the Christian tradition alone. What kind of sickness is this, we may ask? It has recently been described as "our assertive confidence in the superiority of reason. . . ." "We are", as Milton Mayer has said, " 'vestigial Greeks'. . . . We adhere to knowledge, but we cut ourselves off from the mysticism that threaded Greek rationalism. We dying Greeks undertake to prove we-care-not-what by reason alone; and we succeed; and our success in the end undoes us."**

The message of Jung's stone, like the healing influence of Jung's peculiar personality upon the many patients who came

---

*I studied this pattern in the myths of death and rebirth, and set forth the material in *The Wisdom of the Serpent*: The Myths of Death, Rebirth and Resurrection, New York: G. Braziller, 1963, written in collaboration with Miss Oakes.

**An editorial from *Manas*, May 22, 1964. "The Acquirement of Personality."

to him during his long life, proclaims the still-living force of that earlier tradition derived from the original image of the healing art. This is an art that naturally accepts the principle that health is the product of inner change. In terms of Jung's actual formulations, it is to be achieved not by a scientific fragmentation of thought, not by *analysis*, but by *synthesis*, leading to integration.

Therefore, Jung, the analyst, is not represented in this study of his stone. This is quite an appropriate approach to the side of him that is represented by his life at the house in Bollingen. Near the end of Lake Zürich, with the Glärnish Alps for a backdrop, in the seclusion of his garden Jung became what I am afraid his critics would call a mystic, a term he hotly objected to having applied to him. He has given some description of this unique place and its history in his *Memories, Dreams, Reflections*. I trust the careful reader will be able to construe that what it meant to him was not an escape fantasy, but a living part of his philosophy of life and his identity as a pioneer of modern psychology. At Bollingen he first exacted of himself what later he taught his analysands to acquire, and what today hundreds of psychotherapists all over the world enable their patients to use: the ability to give meaningful expression in some art form to the non-rational contents of the unconscious.

It is true, as Jung himself has observed, that this type of creativity initially disturbs the rational mind, and may even seem to embody bad taste when considered from a formal contemporary artistic point of view, but there is no denying its ultimate practical effects. Lewis Mumford, in a review* of Jung's volume of reminiscences, expresses a typical criticism of Jung's psychology as favoring the irrational at the expense of the rational viewpoint, but he observes that Jung in his old age at last reaffirmed the basic validity of the conscious rational mind. What Mr. Mumford can be pardoned for not knowing in this regard, which he would have known if he had seen Jung in his Bollingen mood at a younger age, is that Jung never doubted and never ceased to affirm the basic importance of consciousness. What other reason could there be to create these psychological forms of art if not to make them conscious by seeing

*"The Revolt of the Demons," *The New Yorker*, March 23, 1964.

them, by meditating on their meanings and ultimately integrating the messages they bring?

Jung would also have said that there may be a danger in making conscious the contents of the unconscious before one has participated fully and long in the poetic or religious imagery it expresses. In his English-language seminars in Zürich, where he discussed the meaning of dream and fantasy material, which he subjected to the most searching scientific analysis, he insisted that we must feel the material thoroughly before trying to interpret it. Having allowed the imagery to work upon our feelings, intuitions, and sensations, we could begin to formulate our thoughts about it. Thus he affirmatively urged his students both to learn how to experience the unconscious and how to detach from it, how to experience its universality and then to formulate its specific meaning for the person in whom it manifested itself.

Jung expressed these differing points of view in his comment to Miss Oakes when her project ultimately led her to write her version of the meaning of the symbolism of his stone. In his reaction to reading the first version of the manuscript, he voiced concern that her formulation might sound like the expression of a Jungian dogma. He wrote ". . . [Y]ou understand the stone as a statement about a more or less limitless world of thought-images. I quite agree with your view. One can read the symbols like that. When I hewed the stone I did not think, however. I just brought into shape what I saw on its face."

Miss Oakes states that following her receipt of this letter, she abandoned any thought of publishing her work on the stone and regarded it purely as the expression of a personal experience, to be kept and possibly shared with a few sympathetic friends. In order to make the manuscript more intelligible and readable for this purpose, she rewrote it in the light of Jung's comments. Two years later she sent the final version to him, and in reply he indicated his approval. "Well, you've done it!" he wrote. She still did not attempt to publish it, and turned to other things.

Two years later Jung died. In the week following his death, a television program from New York carried Jerome Hill's color film showing several interesting pictures of the stone, its place at Bollingen, Jung in his stone-cutter's apron and goggles, and finally Jung's brief description of the stone. This unfinished film had originally been intended as a companion piece to Jerome Hill's other two biographical film studies, one about Grandma Moses and the other about Albert Schweitzer. The film about Jung may have been abandoned for the same reason that Miss Oakes abandoned the publication of her study—from a recognition of Jung's own reluctance, while he still lived, to share the treasures of his private garden with the world.

Many years have passed since that time, and Jung has posthumously shown his willingness to open to the world some of the secret places of his inner life with a frankness, a lack of defensiveness, unmatched in any other autobiography of our time. Again, Miss Oakes thought of her study of the stone and generously offered it to me to use as I saw fit, perhaps as an adjunct to my work as a teacher and training analyst. This appealed to me, especially as I had found that a number of my students reacted with great interest to the brief showing of the film about Jung and the stone. But when I read Miss Oakes's manuscript, I felt that it should not be kept for such a limited purpose—that it could perform its teaching function, and something more than that, if it could appear before a larger public. Accordingly, I agreed to write this introduction.

From a pedagogical viewpoint, the relevance of Miss Oakes's study of Jung's stone lies in its providing an excellent example of what we analytical psychologists mean by *amplification*. What Freud described in the basic methodology of psychoanalysis as *free association*, Jung, in the methodology of analytical psychology, called *amplification*. In her description of the stone, Miss Oakes has explained the difference in Jung's psychology between the personal unconscious and the collective unconscious. The personal unconscious contains certain complexes that can be made conscious in an analytical situation by means of free association. In this respect, a Jungian analysis still contains something of the old Freudian method of free association. However, Jung grew dissatisfied with the exclusive use of this method, because he found the free associations, whatever the dream content may have been, always led back to the same typical complexes which in any given case were already known after the initial period of trial analysis was over. Accordingly, he believed that a more discriminating method of interpretation was called for by which the analyst could carry the associations concerning unconscious material to a greater depth, to reveal what might be still unknown.

Jung's rule, which he emphasized in his teaching, might be stated as follows: "You have not interpreted a dream or fantasy correctly if you merely tell the patient something he already knows. Only if you can enable him to learn something about himself he does not know, and this knowledge can be verified as indispensable for the progress of his therapy, has your interpretation succeeded." Accordingly, in many cases this knowledge of the working of the complexes in the personal psyche comes to an end before therapy is completed. In spite of the most helpful interpretations of childhood memories, family patterns, and the inner significance of interpersonal relationships, many an analysis reaches a stalemate.

Jung's first knowledge of the archetypes of the unconscious burst upon him from his own inner experience. He soon saw that if this kind of material were to be used therapeutically in his analytical practice, it required a special method of interpretation. He could not expect from his patients what he expected from himself, which was nothing less than becoming a true scholar specializing in the study of comparative mythology and the history of religions. Yet he soon found that some acquaintance with the mythological parallels to their own unconscious material helped certain patients immensely, and rescued them from the stasis of the condition that depended solely on the method of free association.

In gathering mythological data of this kind, the patient's personal response to his quest was just as important as his knowledge of the material itself. It came about that each individual's version of the mythological pattern he studied was different from any other. Its value for him lay in this very lack of conformity to academic procedures. Yet it also became apparent that unless the mythological study thus undertaken honored the work already done by scholars to classify or elucidate the original material, the results did not ultimately satisfy nor were they productive of further material. Also, a piece of amplification should not be too long or become too involved. There is no end to the study of mythology, since the archetypal images by their very nature become confused and their outlines blurred if too exhaustive a study is attempted.

When, as Miss Oakes clearly demonstrates in her account of Jung's stone, the analysand provides the relevant mythological data, including such references as bits of modern poetry or social conditions among differing peoples or scientific discoveries, and then makes use of this material to illuminate the whole by an individual feeling of its immediate relevance to the modern experience of the archetype, then we have the method of amplification applied as it should be. Amplification anticipates but is not yet interpretation. Nothing has been explained, nothing is to be explained in a literal sense, but a specific insight naturally emerges from such a method that allows the analysand to know something he did not know before. He may be able to formulate this still further, or he may prefer to let it remain as it is. This depends somewhat upon his or her characterological type, i.e., whether he or she is strong in perceptive functioning or in cognitive functioning.

What especially pleases me about Miss Oakes's amplification is that although she is respectful of the scholarly approach and adept at finding her way to the most relevant sources of knowledge of symbolism, she keeps her discussion on a subjective level of feeling for the particular value of the images, in accordance with her psychological disposition. Yet she clearly seeks to understand and to some extent to explain to herself the meaning of the symbolism as she goes along, as an exercise of her thinking function. Finally, her study of Jung's stone shows, as she says, the nature of a "transference," leading her to understand symbolic form as a sense of wholeness or completion that includes what is most relevant without needing to systematize it.

A final word for the skeptical! Jung has often emphasized in his writings that products of the unconscious can only be genuine if they are spontaneous and, according to one commentator, "must not have been acquired through education, tradition, language or indirectly via religious ideas. . . ."* This critic finds this point of view "quite impossible to substantiate," and points out that Jung himself "seems to forget his own stringent criteria, as when he relates how the archetypal nature of an image in one of his own dreams became clear to him when he read of one similar theme in one alchemical treatise . . ." and so forth.

*The Archetypes of the Collective Unconscious, C. G. Jung Review by R. F. Hobson, Journal of Analytical Psychology, Vol. 6. No. 2, July 1961, p. 166.

It is quite true that some inconsistency comes to light here. Far from being uninfluenced, the signs, symbols, and literary elements carved upon Jung's stone could only have been assembled by one whose mind and imagination were deeply influenced by Greco-Roman religious ideas and the symbolism of astrology. Yet Jung maintains that he did arrive at this symbolism spontaneously. "I just brought into shape what I saw on its face," he wrote. At the same time, these symbols are, he says, "attempts to formulate, to define, to shape the inexpressible. . . ." How can such antithetical statements be reconciled?

I think Miss Oakes's amplification of the symbolism of Jung's stone goes a long way toward showing why these statements were not antithetical for Jung himself and why they need not be for anyone who can enter into the creative spirit of such an enterprise. No true artist, such as Jung was at the time of carving his stone, needs to ask himself where the materials of his creation come from or why they come from such divergent sources. This may set a task for the scientist later on. I do think that Jung's own scientific achievement allows us to say that it is practically impossible, except in small children or rare cases of psychosis in the uneducated, to find absolutely pure unconscious material that has been uninfluenced by the cultural past or the cultural environment.

There is, however, a very great difference between these two realms, the cultural past and the cultural environment. Material derived from the cultural environment is suspect because it has largely been introjected from various educational procedures brought to bear upon the individual, without his conscious wish or consent. What comes to him from the cultural past is more reliable because, if really pertinent, he has had to discover it for himself from little-known historical sources of information. If his response to history is genuine and sufficiently profound, he will, like Jung, be influenced only by what he can inwardly sanction as being valid for him. From this point of view, it would be the most natural thing in the world for Jung to find in an alchemical treatise a clarification of one of his own dreams, just as Miss Oakes found in the symbolism of Jung's stone a culturally evocative experience not originally her own.

I have found it useful in my work to distinguish two basic layers of the collective unconscious at successive distances from the consciously observing ego. One is the cultural unconscious; the deepest layer is the primordial unconscious. The cultural unconscious comes to life and to consciousness thanks to the stimulation of an historically oriented education; the primordial unconscious is with us always, and is the layer essentially untouched by cultural changes. Jung's stone has the finished appearance of a product elaborated from the cultural unconscious, but we know from his account of childhood memories and early fantasies that he had many direct encounters with the primordial unconscious.

These primordial experiences were, in Jung's case, strong enough to destroy, for him, the entire edifice of the Christian culture into which he was born. When such a thing happens (and we see it frequently in our analytical practice), the individual so affected may react in one of three distinct ways. He may become demoralized, or psychotic, or learn to regard himself as having sunk to a primitive level from which he has to grow back up through history, exactly as if he had to start all over from the beginning.

Jung tells us of his youthful experiment with primitive fetishism, of his discovery of the religious archetypes, of his rediscovery of Christianity as he emerged into culture-consciousness again. Such an experience of primal things is like an initiation, as Miss Oakes indicates, which conditions its possessor to see everything as if for the first time, spontaneously and originally. Thus even the archetypal images in their ancient cultural forms may be reexperienced in significant ways without any intellectual falsification.

Jung did not set out to produce a neat diagram of the symbolism of astrology and alchemy. He merely used some of the symbols he had known and studied to represent for him the immediate experience of his own primordial depths at this time of his life, when he was seventy-five years old. His attempt to understand or define the personal meaning of these symbols then merely brings his experience of the collective unconscious into communication with his conscious ego. The attempt was made, presumably, to connect all levels, personal, cultural, and primordial, as if they were all aspects of memory, continuous and intercommunicative.

Miss Oakes's exposition of her own thoughts concerning the

stone enables us to feel this unification of the different levels of experience. We cease to care, as we enter the circle of its inner meaning, whether the stone speaks of unconscious or of conscious matters. Then perhaps, even without being able to see the stone in Jung's garden, the reader might hear it "whisper its misty lore of ancient roots and ancestral lives."

Joseph L. Henderson

Preface

My growth, both inner and outer, commenced when I was born in Seattle, Washington, in 1903. My mother and father were easterners who had moved west when they were first married. My parents, Mr. and Mrs. Walter Oakes, joined a small group of young people; together they bought the pointed end of Bainbridge Island, across the bay from Seattle, and formed a country club where their children grew up together. Seattle became our winter home.

The situation was unique, as the land was isolated from the rest of the island by a deep forest of beautiful trees and farmland. On the other three sides of the point were the sea and Puget Sound. The center of the land was high, dense with trees and ferns, and below the heights lay flat land which later became the golf links. There along the edge of the heights were built the houses and gardens that looked way below onto the flat land edged by the beach, or out to sea. In the high ferns in the center we, the children, made secret huts where we hid from our elders and smoked.

I will never forget two quite different views from our home. Outside my small bedroom window grew a climbing rose bush. Here hummingbirds made their nest each year; from my bed next to the window I could observe the nest life without being seen. On the other side of the house toward the south we had a superb view of Mt. Rainier. Snow-capped, it sat in the distant landscape with the serenity of a Buddha. Through absorbing this nature that lay all about me and growing up with friends my age, I observed and experienced a great deal that helped me in later life. This first growth in nature, both negative and positive, took place in my first seven years, from 1903 to 1910, when my father died.

When he died I thought of my own birth, and remembered what my mother had told me. She said that I had nearly died shortly after birth because of enormous hives that had spread over my body and inside my throat, causing it almost to close. As soon as I was put on a formula I recovered. This certainly showed a potent allergy to my mother's milk.

Liticia, a Scandinavian woman, became my nurse. She was short and fat with a large bosom in which she would press me with suffocating hugs. I hated her, as her hugs frightened me and froze my feelings. After a year Liticia went insane and was taken to Stillicum, an asylum for crazy people, where she was incarcerated.

I only remember one dream during that seven-year period. I was standing in a large circle. A steam roller entered it and came toward me. An evil man was driving it, and I was petrified with fear and awoke. It seemed that I would not stop screaming, so my father spanked me until I stopped. This hurt my feelings, as I loved him.

When I was about four my grandparents came from New York City to visit us. My grandfather was tall and handsome, with a luxurious beard. My mother said to him, "Fletcher, don't disturb Maud. She is in her crib and you will scare her with your beard." He did not answer, and entered my room. Leaning down over the bars of the crib, he greeted me with a smile. I looked at him and said, "Boo." From then on we were great friends.

Around this time Cecilia, or Cece, became our nurse-governess. She was half English and Irish, warm and loving, and extremely well educated. She became part of our family, and stayed with us many years. I loved her more than my mother.

My life became very busy as I learned to ride and swim. My teacher was my father, whom I loved. My brother Tom, who was older than me by three years, hated to ride and was scared to swim. This upset my father. I don't remember my sister at all.

Cece had taken my mother's place. I went to Miss Cornish Kindergarten School. During the year the mothers were invited by Miss Cornish to hear the children recite poems. I cried when I recited a poem about a cow that read, "The cow I love with all my heart, she walked about the meadow grass, and wet the meadow flowers." I had substituted "wet" instead of "ate."

My father became very ill with cancer. Tommy and I stayed in the country with Cece. We were taken to see Father lying in a large double bed. He looked so thin and pale that I knew he was very ill, and felt very sad. One night I dreamt that my father walked out the door of the town house and waved good-bye to me and rose into the sky. I woke Cece and told her the dream. It was 6 A.M., so we stayed abed. Around eight the trained nurse called and told Cece that my father had died around 4 A.M.

Several days later we were taken to the funeral that was held in the town house. Later that day my mother sent for me. She was dressed in black with white around the collar, and was seated at the end of the oval dining room table. I stood alone at the other end. When my mother asked me to come to her, I refused and held my hands in back of me. Unconsciously blaming Father's death on Mother, I felt no love for my mother, not realizing that she was very introverted and could not express her feelings.

For a time I was sent to St. Nicholas School, and my brother went to public school. I took painting classes from Mark Toby, a wonderful teacher. Then we moved to New York City and Mother bought an apartment on Park Avenue, No. 62. That summer she took Tom and me to Europe for two months. When we returned, I went to Miss Chapin's School; I was the only westerner.

We returned each summer to our island home in Puget Sound. Often we would go camping in the Olympic Mountains, sleeping under the stars and fishing all day without seeing another human being. It was an experience engraved in my memory.

Maud Oakes

CHAPTER
I

Disaster

I was lying on the terrace after lunch. The hot sun of southern France beat down, tempered with a breeze from the Mediterranean. I felt relaxed, and curiously expectant. I thought how grateful I was to my cousin Jerome Hill for inviting me here to recuperate after my disastrous trip to Peru. I was practically well again.

Hearing footsteps on the path leading from the house, I opened my eyes. It was Jerome. He had a letter in his hand and was smiling.

"From Zürich," he said, waving it.

I sat up. "From Erica?"

He nodded. Erica Anderson was a photographer who had worked with Jerome on two previous award-winning documentaries, one on Grandma Moses and one on Albert Schweitzer.

"Well, what does she say? Has Dr. Jung consented to see you? When? May I go, too?"

"Wait a minute, Maud! One question at a time." He laughed and read me the letter.

Dr. Jung had graciously consented to meet with Jerome in Switzerland regarding the film my cousin was planning. They had hoped to make a documentary of the life and work of C. G. Jung, but in the end only a small amount of footage was completed, owing to difficulties in their professional relationship.

"Here is the date, and I see no reason why you shouldn't come, too. We'll leave Tuesday."

I could hardly contain my anticipation. I had read some of

Dr. Jung's books and had also heard him speak a few years before in New York. I felt great admiration for him, and looked forward to the privilege of meeting him in person with more enthusiasm than I'd felt for a long time—ever since Peru, in fact.

The Peru experience in 1951 had been traumatic and catastrophic. When I received a fellowship from the Bollingen Foundation to explore Peru and Ecuador in search of an isolated village where the Indians still practiced their ancient religion, I was elated. I had done similar work in Guatemala six years before, and it had been very rewarding. After my initial joyous reaction to the Peru opportunity, however, several weeks before my departure I began to grow increasingly uneasy, and had had an inexplicable urge to cancel the whole venture, despite the elaborate plans that had already been made.

I was at that time living contentedly in Big Sur on the central California coast. On the day before I was scheduled to leave for Lima, Peru, I had returned to Big Sur from a trip to Carmel, where I had made my will and completed final preparations for the journey. On my door I found an urgent note from my neighbor, Henry Miller, the well known writer. He said that he needed to see me before I left. I have always believed that whatever comes to me in a natural manner has a special significance for me. It might come in the form of a gift, or an object such as a leaf, shell, stone, or cloud shape. It might be a feeling of apprehension or joy, or even a misfortune. It might be a fantasy, a dream, or even words. I call these happenings "Openers of the Door," and I like to imagine an invisible thread attached to each of them, like the threads attached to the presents at the spider-web birthday parties that we used to have as children. Each of us was given the end of a string that eventually led out of a maze of other strings to an individual gift.

Henry Miller said, "I have been debating whether or not to give you the message I received this morning. As I sat at my work table thinking over my plans for the day, a voice spoke to me saying, 'I have a message for Maud Oakes.' On the other side of the table I saw an elderly woman resembling Madame Blavatsky [the famous psychic] who had come to me before in fantasy. Her message was that if you went to Peru you would experience danger, despair, destruction, disillusionment, and disaster. In the end, however, things would change and there would be some kind of marriage."

Henry was disturbed about giving me such a message, which would naturally upset me. After he left, hesitantly wishing me good luck, I wrote the message on the only available paper, a laundry list. It was then that I noticed that all the words of the warning began with the letter D. I wondered whether death had been part of the message that he had left out.

There was no doubt in my mind about the truth of what Henry had told me. Whether he had dreamed the message or had actually received it from the mysterious woman was not important. The warning more than confirmed my uneasy feelings about the voyage. The voice within said, You must not go. Cancel the whole thing. My mind said, It is too late to give up your Fellowship from the Bollingen Foundation; the jeep is already on its way to Peru, as well as all your camera equipment. Besides, your house is rented. You will have to go.

So I went to Peru. No wonder my short stay there was a disaster—quite the opposite of my earlier three years of experience in Guatemala, where everything had opened for me in an amazing way.

When I had first moved into the Guatemalan Indian village of Todos Santos, where I lived for eighteen months in 1945 and 1946 with the Mam Indians, an inner voice had suggested that I burn five candles in the tiny church: four to their Mayan gods of the mountaintops and one to my God. I asked for their protection and help. Also, I prayed that I might remain open to receive. I had many difficult experiences, but I accepted them, for inwardly I felt that they were tests I had to meet and experience in this life, somewhat similar to the ancient initiations. I was often lonely, but seldom really frightened; I felt that I was in the hand of God and therefore protected.

But in Peru I felt vulnerable—very much alone and not at all protected. Although I was keenly aware of the beauty of Lima, "City of the Kings," and had ample time to visit the fascinating museums and private collections full of extraordinary ancient Indian art and culture, I was nevertheless in despair and became increasingly nervous and negative. Everything went wrong in Peru. My camera equipment was held up by customs. The jeep station wagon arrived late, minus some of its equipment. I began to wonder what was going to happen next.

Sometimes I walked the mysterious streets in the cool evening, admiring the Spanish architecture and decorative iron work, noticing the Indian faces of the passersby. I thought of their great Inca civilization, later conquered and destroyed by Spanish treachery and greed. Some streets held the scent of garden flowers; others were full of the smell of rancid cooking oil and tropical decay. As I walked along, I often had strange thoughts and feelings. Where am I? I asked myself. Is this really Lima? Am I Maud Oakes, and why am I here? I felt completely out of time, and when I thought of Henry's warning written on the laundry list, which I carried with me, I was fearful.

Of the ancient cultures of Peru, the mother culture, Chavin, appealed to me most. The stone carvings were amazing in technique and full of symbolism of the serpent, which fascinated me. So when the jeep and camera equipment finally arrived, I decided to go on my first trip.

The road led over the high Cordilleras to the towns of Huaras and Monterey, near Chavin ruins. I was accompanied by Carmen, the charming daughter of the Peruvian family whom I was visiting. Her mother had asked me to take her with me. Young and energetic, she proved to be a delightful companion.

On the third of April, 1951, Carmen and I started out in the jeep station wagon. When we obtained our police permit at the Lima AAA office, we were told that our trip to Monterey would take four hours. (Later we discovered by bitter experience that the journey usually took ten hours.)

From Lima we went northward on a highway cut into the side of a mountain of grey sand. The Pacific Ocean lay far below on one side, and sand trickled down onto the road from an almost perpendicular slope on the other. The Indian road crews were kept busy clearing sand from the highway. After a while, the sandy incline leveled out into a coastal desert—a veritable sea of sand, its moving forms sculpted by the winds. This desert was broken at infrequent intervals by bright green oases watered by a mountain stream. Aside from these oases, the colors of the desert landscape were shades of beige and grey, which gave me a feeling of sadness and death. Not a blade of grass or a living thing was to be seen. It was as I imagined one of the circles of Dante's Inferno to be. I had read that the ancient Peruvians had buried their dead along this coastal desert north and south of Lima. Millions of skeletons had been discovered in the tombs of the ancient sand cemeteries. Long concealed by the sands and preserved by desiccation, amazing treasures had been found in excellent condition.

After about three hours of following the coast, we turned off the highway toward the high mountains. The narrow dirt road wound tortuously through a valley watered by a small river bordered by haciendas of sugar cane. Leaving the valley behind, we climbed upward through stark, forbidding mountain terrain devoid of vegetation. I felt I was on a road of test and trial, completely out of time.

After several hours of climbing, we entered a landscape of beautiful trees that covered the mountains. The road became steeper, and we met several trucks. At a small pueblo of about three houses, we stopped for gas. It was only after much persuasion on the part of Carmen, with her beautiful pleading black eyes, that the reluctant owner sold us some. To our amazement, the man told us that we had about five hours more of driving before we would arrive in Monterey. Why I never considered spending the night there and sleeping in the jeep is beyond my comprehension. This was my first mistake, especially since I was responsible for Carmen. It was almost as if I had an unconscious inner drive that compelled me to go on. Although the rainy season was considered to be over, with darkness came the rain. I put the jeep into low gear and four-wheel drive, since the road was slippery and in bad repair, with frightening sheer drops. Our machine climbed like a goat. The rain fell steadily in this wild land. We took pills for altitude sickness, knowing that the pass ahead of us was thirteen thousand feet high. I drove very slowly, my headlights revealing that near the edge, which dropped off into a black abyss, the dirt road was washed out in places. At around eight-thirty the road leveled off, and we knew we had reached the *puno*, the top of the pass.

Suddenly the lights of the jeep went out: I pulled over to the inside of the road and stopped. With my flashlight I tried without success to locate the short. The motor was all right, but none of the lights worked. We sat in the rain and darkness, wrapped in our coats. I was worried, knowing that we were in a very wild part of the country.

In a short time, however, a huge truck came along, going in our direction. The driver could hardly believe that there were two women all alone on this little-traveled road. By my flashlight

I could see that he was an older man with a very handsome Roman-like Inca profile. Unable to fix the short, he warned us that the night would grow much colder, but added that the road would soon descend, and in about an hour and a half we would reach the nearest town. He advised me to follow him, saying he would drive very slowly and that, if things were not right, I could blow my horn, and he would hear me.

I knew that it would be dangerous to follow him, since he had only one dim red rear light. But I also realized that we could not spend the night alone at thirteen thousand feet without blankets or winter coats, so I decided to follow him. Maybe this was my second mistake.

He proceeded at about ten miles an hour, and I stayed about five feet in back of his truck, since I could see nothing but the small red light. After about half an hour, Carmen crawled to the back of the jeep to sleep. Thank God she did.

In the darkness and rain I kept following the truck. Wherever the little red light moved, I followed. Our jeep seemed like a trailer, attached to another vehicle by an invisible cord of concentration. Carmen was in the land of dreams. I began to wonder, what kind of a land am I in? Where am I going? I tried to comfort myself with a saying of the Navaho Indians: "You will know where you are going when you get there."

Suddenly I felt the right front wheel slip into space, into a dreadful nothingness. It was as if we were falling in an elevator. To the appalling sounds of metal grinding against rock and frightening crashes, the car turned over and over.

"So this is it!" I cried. I was sure it was my end. Then came a long silence when the jeep at last hit bottom and came to rest. I called out "Carmen!" and she called "Matilda!" We were alive and could speak and move. It was a miracle.

I became aware of the frightening odor of gasoline. I had been thrown into the rear of the car, which was now resting on its side. I managed to crawl forward in the darkness, feeling my way over the baggage, and turned off the motor. I found my overcoat, which I had come out of as I fell, my pocketbook, and also Carmen's shoes, which she had lost, but no flashlight. Although Carmen had matches, we dared not use them because of the leaking gas. I felt something very sticky on my hands and wondered if it were blood. (Later we discovered it was strawberry jam.)

As the smell of gas grew stronger, we tried to get out. It was terrifying. We felt trapped, for jagged glass was everywhere. All the windows had been broken, except for half a sliding one which we finally managed to pull back. We squeezed through it and pulled ourselves onto the upturned side of the car. Here we sat for a moment, and I suggested that we give thanks to God and the gods of the mountains that we were alive. I had found splinters of glass even in my mouth, so I climbed down to the river to wash my mouth. I also washed my eyes, for I had felt something in them and feared that this too might be glass. Later it proved to be only sand.

In the darkness we could at least see that the jeep was resting on a hugh rock, probably granite, next to a small river. We were in the bottom of a ravine. Although the slope was very steep, it was nothing compared to the sheer cliffs we had seen earlier. We realized again how extremely fortunate we were. With legs weakened by shock and altitude, we managed to struggle, slipping and scrambling, up the steep slope, which was lined with rocks and blocks of granite.

Stepping onto the road was like stepping from the unknown, frightening netherworld into the beautiful enfolding world of nature and man. The rain had ceased, and the sky was filled with bright, friendly stars. As we gazed about us, I thought, Here we stand on the top of the world. How deeply thankful I am to the gods of these high mountains. I had completely forgotten Henry Miller and his message.

Carmen had been wonderful throughout our harrowing experience, never losing her head, but now she began to shake all over from shock and cold. We joined arms and walked up and down to keep warm. After a while I began to laugh, and Carmen asked why. "Your first vacation. What a vacation!" I answered, and we both laughed hysterically.

Half an hour later another truck appeared with three men, going in the opposite direction. When we pointed down into the ravine, and their powerful flashlight illuminated our smashed jeep far below, they were speechless—overwhelmed with wonder that we were alive and walking. Seeing that we were wet and cold and still in a state of shock, they gave us several swigs of brandy from the cargo they were carrying. They were all young and helpful. I could not see them clearly, partly because of the effects of the brandy, but chiefly because of the darkness that enveloped us. By their headlights we could all see the wheel marks of the truck I had been following and where the truck had swerved to the side of the road to avoid a deep hole. The driver had probably forgotten momentarily that we were following him. It was safe for his truck with four rear wheels, but not for us. The tracks showed my right wheel had sunk into a soft, washed-out place near the edge, which had given way, toppling us over.

The driver told us that we were in luck—a passenger bus would soon be going by in our direction. He advised us to take it, since there would not be another bus till morning. The men started unloading our jeep, saying the car would be stripped by thieves before morning if they didn't remove our things. Before they had finished, the bus arrived. It had to stop to avoid hitting the truck, which the truck driver had moved across the road. The bus driver was not in the least concerned about our accident, us, or with waiting a few minutes for the rest of our baggage to be brought up from below. He said he would not accept us because he had a woman passenger aboard who would die if he did not get her to the nearest doctor. But our friendly driver refused to move his truck until we were safely inside the bus with all our luggage. There was no vacant seat, nor the offer of one, so we had to sit on our suitcases in the aisle. The one-hour ride with no springs proved to be most uncomfortable for Carmen and agonizing for me. It was then that I realized that the base of my spine had been injured.

We left the bus at the first town, and there we found our truck driver guide. How nice it was to see his friendly Inca face. When he saw us he crossed himself, and when he heard what had happened he blamed himself. He had never missed us, he said, until he had arrived at the town. He was planning to return to see what had happened. With his aid we reported the accident to the police and hired some men to pull the jeep out of the ravine before thieves could remove the tires and other equipment.

There was no hotel in the town, so the helpful Inca driver offered to take us to Huaras. We reached Huaras at four-thirty, but found no rooms available in the one small hotel. He took us on to Monterey, twenty minutes away. There we found a very nice, clean hotel run by a Swiss hotelkeeper. The driver refused to accept payment for his transportation. He repeated that our misfortune had been his fault, and if we had been killed, it would have been on his head. When we reached our rooms, we both swallowed a slug of brandy and two aspirins. We were so tired that we removed only our shoes and coats and fell into bed.

The next morning I could hardly move, and it was impossible to sit up. The room boy propped me up in bed and brought me breakfast. Carmen came in, and we took stock of our injuries. She had a cut on her ear and foot and a very bad bruise on her hip. Since she had been in the back of the jeep, she had suffered little compared to me, and for this I was grateful. I had two bad bumps on my head, my neck felt out of joint, and my body was a mass of bruises, but by far the most painful injury was to my rear end. It was agony even to try to sit or get up. Particles of glass were still in my hair and down my back. My eyes were inflamed, but there was no glass in them, only sand.

From then on, things changed for the better because of four young geologists who were staying at the hotel. They took care of us, and one of them fell in love with Carmen. They hired a car to return us to Lima the next day, and also saw that our wrecked jeep was towed to Lima a few days later. Our return to Lima took ten and a half hours, all of them agonizing for me. En route, we stopped the car to see where we had gone off the road. We saw with amazement that we had plummeted seventy-five feet into the ravine. We were overwhelmed with gratitude for having escaped death.

In the American hospital in Lima, spinal x-rays were taken from my neck down, and treatments were administered by a doctor recommended by Carmen's mother. Then the Foundation cabled me to return to New York.

As I sat on a rubber ring in the New York-bound plane, Henry's message hit me with great force. I had already experienced despair, danger, destruction, and disaster. What lay ahead, he had said, were disillusionment and "some kind of marriage." The disillusionment did come later, although it does not concern this story. As for some kind of marriage, it proved to be very different from what I had expected and is, in fact, the theme of this book.

CHAPTER
II

The Beginning

I arrived in New York in the middle of April 1951. The whole rhythm of the city, together with the people I met, seemed to belong to a world apart. Further x-rays revealed that I had a fractured vertebra in my neck and a bent coccyx. Although I felt very sorry for myself, I was thankful that I had escaped with such relatively minor injuries. After several months of orthopedic treatment, I went to recuperate at the home of my cousin, Jerome Hill, in Cassis in the South of France. My doctor felt that the best medicine for me was a complete rest in the sun, with swimming to keep my spine in alignment. He was right, because gradually I began to feel better physically.

But as I swam in the clear Mediterranean sea and lay in the hot southern sun, my thoughts kept returning to Peru. I felt deeply that there must be a lesson to be learned from my disastrous Peruvian adventure. Gradually, I began to see that my attitude had changed without my having been aware of it. In my previous work with Navaho and Mam Indian shamans and medicine men, I had accepted all that I experienced with them as part of my own personal initiation pattern. When I faced what came with humility, inner strength, and understanding, each experience or test had been a step forward on my path. Questioning myself now, I suddenly saw that I must have felt that my initiation had been completed. I decided that Henry Miller must have sensed what had been happening, and had been used unconsciously to warn me that I was endangering my own maturing womanhood with a closed, "know it all" attitude in relation to

11

my Peruvian journey. Furthermore, I had not listened to my inner voice that told me not to depart, and had ignored my feelings of apprehension. I had wilfully disregarded the "Openers of the Door." No wonder everything had turned against me.

Having evolved this understanding, my interests presently turned from Peru and southern France to Switzerland and to Dr. Jung. I had read several of Jung's books and had attended one of his lectures, so my cousin's project interested me very much. When I was invited to go with him and Erica to call on Jung at his country retreat near Bollingen, I was pleased at the thought of meeting the famous man, even though, because of an unfortunate past experience, I had misgivings about Jungian analysis or, indeed, any kind of analysis. Although there was much to see and enjoy in the short visit with Dr. and Mrs. Jung, it was Jung himself, and especially what he had carved on the central face of a stone placed in his walled garden, that captured me and remained most clearly in my thoughts.

I remember walking through the arch of a stone wall that separated his house from an exterior terrace, and seeing there the stone Jung had just finished carving, sitting on its foundation in the most important place in the garden. It stood out starkly against its surroundings and rather resembled, I thought, a newly placed tombstone at the foot of a lone tree. Like a magnet it drew me toward it. I wondered if the tree symbolized growth into life and consciousness, and the stone—a tombstone—death, death for rebirth. I saw clearly its carved face. My eyes concentrated on the little hooded, childlike figure centered in the mandala design, and immediately I felt as if the child were a well known friend.

Reluctantly pulling myself away from the mysterious little bas-relief figure, I joined the others on a tour of the garden and house, conducted by Dr. Jung. The kitchen, with its large circular floor, fascinated me. I wondered how Mrs. Jung coped with this primitive kitchen, where the only way to cook was over charcoal, and all water had to be pumped from an outdoor well. Before we reached the entrance hall, I prayed that Dr. Jung would allow us to see his study. As we stood in the hall preparing to leave, he turned to me and to another guest who had joined the tour and asked if we would like to visit his study. I climbed the stairs in excitement, and was shown into a very small round room located in the tower. As I remember, Jung's desk fitted into the curved wall. Opposite, within reach of his hands, were manuscripts, books, and vellum-bound alchemical treatises and, on the wall, a Tibetan *tanka* and all kinds of objects for making magic.

Six months later I was back in New York, hospitalized with a recurrence of amoebic dysentery contracted in Peru, when Erica Anderson showed me a small photograph she had taken of the mandala-face of Jung's carved Stone. It seemed to jump out at me! There was no doubt that it was an "Opener of the Door." It spoke to me and seemed to say, "I am a Stone that heals, makes whole, if you become aware of my significance for you." I felt its power and knew—profoundly knew—that I must try to discover the meaning of its carvings. At that time, the powerful effect of the design on one who lacked energy and interest was amazing. It was like turning on the light in a dark, stale room.

When he heard about my potent reaction to the mandala, my cousin Jerome gave me the job of trying to analyze the meaning of Jung's Stone for use in his film on Jung. When I returned to my Big Sur home to convalesce, Jerome sent me a copy of Jung's statement about the Stone, together with a two-foot-high enlarged photograph of its face with the circular design.

The only clues that I had to begin with were a few words of Jung's recorded on tape. Jung said:

> It was one of many cut stones that had come from the quarry across the lake. The foreman superintending the unloading of the barge noticed amongst the cargo a large cubic stone that had not been ordered. Angrily, the foreman told the men working for him that the stone must be returned to the quarry. When I arrived at the scene at this moment and noticed the Stone rejected by the builders, it struck my fancy and I leapt upon it, with the decision not only to keep it but to carve its surface.

Over a period of two years, in his spare moments, Jung carved the Stone and when it was finished gave it the place of honor in his walled garden.

It is a cube of grey sandstone measuring about a foot and a half in height, width, and depth. Only three of the four sides are carved. Jung's words on the tape continued:

> On the center face of the Stone, it is a large circle within a square. Inside this circle is a much smaller circle, like the hub

of a wheel, and within the hub stands a figure. It is dressed in a hood with a short cape and on its body is the sign of the planet Mercury. In its left hand is a lantern and the right hand seems to be pointing. From the inner circle radiate outward four diagonal lines, three of them zig-zag and one undulating like a river or a serpent, dividing the wheel into four equal parts. This one, the river, had a double meaning, the alchemist's secret, the axioma of Maria the Prophetess. In the part to the [viewer's] left is the sun; in the part to the right, the moon. Next to the sun is the sign for the planet Jupiter; in the part above, that of Saturn; next to the Moon, that of Venus; and in the part below, the sign for Mars. Counting the sign of Mercury on the body of the figure in the center, this makes The Sacred Seven of the Ancients —the two luminaries and the five planets.

The four spaces between the inner and outer circles are covered with Greek inscriptions. The following quotations come from Jung's autobiographical book, *Memories, Dreams, Reflections,* wherein he explains the inscriptions more fully. The first says: *"Time is a child—playing like a child—playing a board game— the kingdom of the child."* The second inscription reads: *"This is Telesphorus, who roams through the dark regions of this cosmos and glows like a star out of the depths. He points the way to the gates of the sun and to the land of dreams."*[1]

On the left face of the Stone, the side that faces the lake, is a Latin text that Jung himself composed. He says in his book, *"These sayings are more or less quotations from alchemy."*[2]

> The stone speaks now, being personified of himself and says: I am an orphan, alone; nevertheless I am found everywhere. I am one, but opposed to myself. I am youth and old man at one and the same time. I have known neither father nor mother, because I have had to be fetched out of the deep like a fish, or fell like a white stone from heaven. In woods and mountains I roam, but I am hidden in the innermost soul of man. I am mortal for everyone, yet I am not touched by the cycles of aeons.

On the right face of the Stone is a second Latin text. It is a verse by Arnaldus de Villanova, a famous physician and alchemist of the early thirteenth century, which reads: *"Here stands the mean, uncomely stone, Tis very cheap in price! The more it is despised by fools, the more loved by the wise."* And carved under it are the words: "*C. G. Jung, out of gratitude has made and placed this stone in memory of his seventy-fifth birthday, in the year 1950.*"

During the first year that I meditated on the meaning of the Stone, I realized that even though it was not carved for me, its effect on me was like that of a Navaho sand painting on the patient for whom it is made. I was slowly recovering from my illness. Meditating on the Stone was therapeutic for me, psychically as well as physically. In addition, it provided a necessary focus and discipline. During the next year I continued to work on the Stone and it worked on me. At times it was a difficult and subjective experience not unlike an analysis, for it seemed that I had made a transference to the Stone in the way an analysand transfers expectations for a basic change onto the analyst.

Working on the Stone opened up previously unknown, stimulating horizons; eventually my experience with it became this book. In the course of my work, the completion of the initial manuscript led to my second meeting with Jung, in the late fall of 1953. This time we met at Jung's home in Küsnacht, situated on Lake Zürich, where he saw his patients. Jerome and I made the visit together, he to consult Jung on the possibility of basing a film on my research on the Stone, and I to explore the practicability of using this material for a book, though I did not mention it at the time.

I smile as I remember how upset I was by Jung's remark after he greeted us that day: "My friends, how can I help you? I realize how difficult your task is. The Stone is nothing. I am not an artist; I did it to amuse myself. It is a holiday thing—as if I sang a song."

My heart sank as I heard his words, for the Stone had told me that its carvings might represent the essence of Jung's life experience. I said in a faint voice, "But the Stone is very powerful."

Jung repeated: "How can I help you? I don't know who I am. I am the last person to tell you who I am. I'm invisible. I am nothing; I am an old man. I no longer lie. Once perhaps, I had to, as a young scientist without a reputation. Now I no longer lie. What I have to say is so simple that it is hard to understand; it is refused. It is so far away ahead of now. It cannot be shown to those who do not think. In Switzerland my books seem to reach the most unlikely people—uneducated people. Truth is like water; it passes all barriers."

We were with Jung about an hour and a half, enough time for him to become better acquainted with us. Jerome and Jung did most of the talking, for I was too disturbed by Jung's comments about the Stone. However, I did tell him about a dream I had had while working with a Navaho shaman:

> *I was sitting nude on yellow corn meal in the Wind God's pollen basket. (Yellow corn meal is female; white is male.) The holy Wind God was looking at me.*

When I awoke and recorded the dream, I had wondered whether I should tell the shaman the dream. I had thought, if he thinks it is a bad dream, he might stop working for me.

Jung said, "That old mind," and then asked me what I had done. "I told the shaman my dream," I said, "and since he felt it was a good dream, he sprinkled me with pollen and prayed over me."

We were leaving when Jung said, "I hope I have given you some ideas of what I am." Then he looked directly at me, saying, "I need not have written any books; it is all on the Stone." These words bolstered up my deflated ego and also amused me as I remembered his remarks: "I am an old man; I no longer lie."

Then Jung planted a seed in my mind: "If you wish to consult someone on your work on the Stone," he said, "you could contact Dr. L., an analyst friend of mine, who lives on your side of the world." Then he opened the door and we said our farewells. As we descended the stairs, the door of Jung's study opened again and he called down to us, "Now be sure and let me know what happens. Let me know what you do. I am very curious. I am anxious to know."

Jerome answered, "I have tried to keep you in touch when there was anything to tell about the film. Sometimes things that begin like this, hesitantly and sporadically, suddenly get their growth."

Jung said, as he closed the door, "Yes! Things do happen."

I remember well the letter I wrote to Jung on January 7, 1956, after I had completed the first draft of the next manuscript that evolved from my research on the Stone. I had chosen the seventh because I felt it was a holy number and might bring me luck.

Big Sur, California
January 7, 1956

Dear Dr. Jung:

It is over two years ago that I had the pleasure of visiting you at Küsnacht with my cousin Jerome Hill. On my return home I realized that it was not only impertinent but an impossibility for me to even attempt to say what the designs and inscriptions on the Stone symbolize to you. There was only one way for me to approach the Stone and that was to experience it in myself. Many times since I have felt it was presumptuous of me to attempt such a project for I am not a scholar, not a psychologist, and though I am a painter-writer and an amateur anthropologist, I have no degrees. Just the same I remembered what you said at Küsnacht: "What I have to say is so simple." This statement encouraged me enough to hope that you might be interested in the Stone's effect on an ordinary person. So what I am sending you under separate cover is my own personal experience of the Stone—your Stone. If you have time to read my MS "The Stone Speaks," I would appreciate any suggestions and criticism.

At the end of the month, I received an air mail letter from Zürich which thrilled me so much that I could hardly open the envelope.

Küsnacht, Zürich
January 31, 1956

Dear Miss Oakes,

As you can imagine, I am quite astonished to hear about your project, although I am fully aware of the fact that an imaginative person could easily write not one, but several volumes about my stone. All the volumes I had written are "*in nuce*" contained in it. The mandala itself is just a sort of hieroglyph, hinting at and trying to express a vast background in a most abbreviated form. Your method to realize its contents through your subjective experience is unexceptionable, as a matter of fact the only correct way of reading its message. That is just the virtue of symbolic expression, that it can be read in many different ways by many different individuals. And if they are honest, the reading will be correct. Thus, as you see, I am prepared for the shock to get the MS about a thing most emphatically belonging to my innermost self. I only ask you to be patient with the slow ways of old age—*Deo concedente* you will get an answer.—*Inshallah!*

Then in answer to my manuscript came a wonderful second letter:

Küsnacht, Zürich
February 2, 1956

Dear Miss Oakes,

I have read your meditation about the stone with much interest. Your method of reading its messages is adequate and in this case the only one yielding positive results. You understand the stone as a statement about a more or less limitless world of thought-images. I quite agree with your view. One can read the symbols like that. When I hewed the stone I did not think, however. I just brought into shape what I saw on its face.

Sometimes you express yourself (in the MS), as if my symbols and my text were sort of a confession of a belief. Thus it looks as if I were moving in the vicinity of Theosophy. In America, especially, one blames me for my so-called mysticism. Since I don't claim at all to be the happy proprietor of metaphysical truths, I should prefer that you attribute to my symbols the same tentativeness which characterizes your explanatory attempts. You see, I have no religious or otherwise convictions about my symbols. They can change tomorrow. They are mere allusions, they hint at something, they stammer and often lose their way. They try only to point in a certain direction, viz. to those dim horizons beyond which lies the secret of existence. They are just no Gnosis, no metaphysical assertions. They are partly even futile or dubious attempts at pronouncing the ineffable. Their number therefore is infinite and the validity of each is to be doubted. They are nothing but humble attempts to formulate, to define, to shape the inexpressible. "*Wo fass ich Dich, unendliche Natur?*" (Faust) It is not a doctrine, but a mere expression of and a reaction to the experience of an ineffable mystery.

There is one point more I want to mention: the stone is not a product only of thought images, but just as much of feeling and local atmosphere, i.e., of the specific *ambiente* of the place. The stone belongs to its secluded place between the lake and hill, where it expresses the *beata solitudo* and the *genius loci,* the spell of the chosen and walled-in spot. It could be nowhere else and cannot be thought of or properly understood without the secret web of threads that relate to its surroundings. Only there in its solitude it can say: *Orphanus sum* and only there it makes sense. It is there for its own sake and only seen by a few. Under such conditions only, the stone will whisper its misty lore of ancient roots and ancestral lives.

Thank you for letting me see your typescript.

The night after receiving this letter I dreamt about Jung:

I awoke in a room in the eaves of a house made of wood. Jung was asleep in a bed next to the window. I had two pillows on my bed and I saw that he had only one, so I arose to get him another. Then we were both dressed and about to go to a lecture. He asked me if I worked for the Bollingen Foundation, and I said yes. Jung vanished and I found myself in a square room. A waiter, an evil waiter, was talking on the phone saying, "We will turn the water on until she does what we want her to do." The water began to pour into the room and slowly rise. I thought I should have to swim or drown. I found a large stone and went to the window and with it hit the glass pane a blow and the water poured out.

I felt this dream was a warning that I must not become too much identified with what I thought the Stone symbolized to Jung. I would then be possessed by the evil animus (the waiter) and drown in my own unconsciousness. I must find my own interpretation of the Stone and use it consciously.

When my manuscript was returned, I saw that Jung had corrected it by hand. I was greatly encouraged, for I knew that he would not have bothered to do this unless he had felt the manuscript had value. A few nights later I had another dream:

I was half asleep in a large, limitless bed that stretched into infinity. It was dark and a man's voice called to me and I answered. We asked each other questions and gave answers. I arose and the bed vanished, though I had the same feeling of the landscape stretching in all directions. The man who called came through the darkness and touched me and I knew it was Jung. He said to me: "At last you have come; I have waited for you for a long time; now you have released me and I can go." We embraced and then he left. I found myself out-of-doors with Jung, Mrs. Jung, Jerome, and friends. Jung did not refer to the previous visit. Jung and I in turn immersed an object in water and it floated. Mrs. Jung said: "How did you know?" I said, "I knew when he touched me."

Through my transference to the Stone it became humanized by contact with the man. Jung then became the carrier of the Self for me. Mrs. Jung was a positive feminine figure who as Jung's wife insured that my transference would not be misunderstood as being purely personal. The object we immersed in water floated, meaning that to float was to maintain consciousness while yet remaining in close contact with the unconscious. Did it also show that my experiment with the Stone would float successfully someday?

After working another year on the manuscript, I again sent a copy to Jung for criticism. I also told him that I would be traveling to Switzerland and wondered whether I could visit him at Bollingen. Soon, the coveted invitation arrived.

My spirits soared with anticipation during the hour's drive from Zürich to Bollingen. It was a beautiful clear day. The road passed along the lake and through several attractive villages. There were many beautiful vineyards climbing the hills away from the lake, and tidy farms with flower and vegetable gardens.

The driver of the car did not know the location of Jung's house. Even though six years had passed since I had last visited Bollingen, I remembered certain landmarks and guided us there. Since there was no set path to the house, I left the car and walked toward the lake through a field where two farmers were stacking hay. I could not see the house until I was almost upon it, because of its low situation on the lake with the trees concealing it. The door was set in a high stone wall, where I waited at least five minutes, watching the gracefully swaying reeds that grew near the shore. In this way I observed the etiquette of the Navaho by not announcing myself until I had waited a while outside the door. The pause gave me time to gather myself in order to feel my innermost center.

When the heavy wooden door was opened by a friend of Dr. Jung's and I stepped inside, all preconceived plans fell away. I had passed from one world into another—from a material world of many people into the world of nature in which Jung had created his house at Bollingen.

I saw a bronze sundial that I remembered from before. It was set high on a stone foundation, so that it commanded a wide view of the beautiful lake and mysterious mountains. To my right was the stone house, which was also part of a stone wall that enclosed all but the lake side of the house and garden complex. The house was medieval in feeling, with two towers, and had a singular individuality and elegance. Looking at it, I remembered a dream I had had many years before after hearing Jung give a lecture in New York:

> *I saw a medieval castle with a moat encircling it. There was no water in the moat, but there was a full-blown red rose. I climbed down into the moat and picked up the rose, since I felt it was mine.*

This dream had certainly been an Opener of the Door, but I was not sufficiently conscious then to realize its significance. Now I know that the rose represents wholeness, symbolizing love. So the dream suggests that knowledge of what Jung represents would later bring integration through a new development.

I stood looking about me, and recalled that Jung had bought this land in 1922, ten years after his break with Freud. Jung first designed and built a tower form, influenced by a round hut he had seen in Africa in 1926. This part of the house eventually became a "dwelling tower," wherein Jung worked for thirty-two years while he designed, carved, and built the rest of the house and garden. It was completed in 1955, two years before my present visit.

The completion of the house at Bollingen must have been a long, slow process, in a way resembling the process of analysis. The designing of the house and the stone carvings that Jung fashioned must have been therapeutic for him, as he deeply probed and experienced his own unconscious. I felt that Jung had built two houses in one, his inner house and Bollingen, the latter being an outer expression of an inner process. Moreover, Bollingen was created in the way a true artist creates a work of art. It was done with love, and I felt this.

In Jung's autobiography, published after his death, he speaks of the tower:

> From the beginning I felt the Tower as in some way a place of maturation—a maternal womb or a maternal figure in which I could become what I was, what I am and will be. It gave me a feeling as if I were being reborn in stone. It is thus a concretization of the individuation process, a memorial *aere perennius*. . . . At Bollingen I am in the midst of my true life, I am most deeply myself. . . . At times I feel as if I am spread out over the landscape and inside things, and am myself living in every tree, in the plashing of the waves, in the clouds and the animals that come and go, in the procession of the seasons. There is nothing in the Tower that has not grown into its own form over the decades, nothing with which I am not linked. Here everything has its own history, and mine; here is space for the spaceless kingdom of the world's and the psyche's hinterland.[3]

Walking again through the archway between the house and the terrace, I felt that the setting of Bollingen must hold a special meaning for Jung. It was situated low on the lake, in contrast to the hills and mountains that surrounded it. There was a striking contrast between the walled-in house and garden and the open aspect toward the lake—one side was enclosed, protected, and the other side was completely open to the living lake. Between the two sides—the enclosed and the open, the hills and the lake—stood the Stone.

How different it was from the first time I had seen it six years before, when it had been newly set in the garden! Moss now grew on the inscriptions, and the lone tree was only one of many trees and shrubs. I felt that the way the Stone was placed on its base was a clue to its enigmatic carvings. Much later, Jung told me that the lower level of the foundation was composed of six rocks, the second level of two rocks, and on top of these stood the Stone. I touched it with my hand the way I would a well-loved friend and thought, "You are an Opener of the Door, unlike earlier stones that Jung carved for his house. They were prospective but you are retrospective of what Jung discovered and experienced and what he goes back to in thought."

Next to the Stone, on the lake side, were two comfortable chairs and a bench, the latter a part of the Stone's base. Beyond and jutting out into the water were several rocks. I stepped onto them and stood watching a family of ducks and some swans gliding by and, beyond, an old fisherman rowing past. A voice next to me boomed out in salutation to the fisherman; as I turned around, Jung greeted me. I remember him very clearly. He was a tall, well-built man, slightly stooped because of age. As he looked at me, his eyes were keen and penetrating, with a twinkle in their depths. His mouth was sensitive, humorous, and stubborn, and his whole being conveyed a feeling of simplicity and sincerity, of wisdom and understanding and great kindness. To me he was a combination of scientist, artist, woodsman, and something of the shaman.

We sat in the chairs between the Stone and the lake and had tea. We discussed many things, including the book he was just finishing on flying saucers[4] and my manuscript on his Stone. I asked him whether he believed in the reality of the saucers, or whether he felt they were man's projections, and he answered, "Both."

In reference to my manuscript, Jung said, "Yes, you have done it." When I then asked his permission to publish it, he said, "Yes, in America, but not in Europe until after my death." He then asked me if the Stone had led me into my analysis. I merely nodded my head. I was too shy to explain to Jung that he and the Stone had actually led me into my analysis some years before. Jung, the alchemist, had planted the two necessary seeds, the first at Küsnacht in 1953 when he suggested Dr. L.'s name as a consultant on the Stone, and the second when he wrote to Dr. L. and asked him if he were near Big Sur to call on me and see how my work was coming along. In this way, hardly realizing it, I had been led into a personal analysis—a very necessary experience for me or any person attempting to analyze Jung's carvings on the Stone.

When it was time for me to leave, Dr. Jung and I stood silently gazing at the Stone. He then conducted me to the gate. His last words were a suggestion that I visit the prehistoric caves at Lascaux in France.

My cousin Jerome and I went to Lascaux a month later. I will always be thankful to Dr. Jung for this great experience. The approach to the caves, in a thinly wooded place with no distinguishable view, was not at all what I had imagined. We descended some stairs into the earth and passed through a salesroom. As we walked through the door into the cave, I felt apprehensive. It was somewhat the same feeling I had had when I first began analysis, and that I would have again when I took LSD.

Passing into the Hall of the Bulls, we stepped out of time into a subterranean temple-room of Paleolithic times. As I gazed about me, I could hardly believe that 30,000 years ago *Homo sapiens* (man who discerns) had painted what I now beheld. I realized I was in the presence of the birth of creative art. The strength and vitality of the lifelike drawings were overwhelming. The use of the earth colors was simply executed, and conveyed the feeling of beauty and power. The austere bulls, the watchful reindeer, the bison and the prancing horses were all part of a happy hunting scene. The most arresting figure was the one I first saw as I entered the cave. It has been described as an "imaginary animal, a unicorn." To me he was decidedly a spirit animal, a magic wizard beast, leader of the hunting scene.

The most impressive drawing, in a shaft or well found at the end of a deep passage in the cave, was of a disemboweled charging bison and the only representation of Lascaux Man. Though crudely drawn in black, there was no doubt what he represented. Here lay a man, a spirit man identified with the higher forces, which were shown by his bird mask and his two rods of power—his erect phallus and his staff of office surmounted by a bird's head. The drawing certainly illustrated a sacred magical rite. It showed not only that Lascaux Man was a creative artist who could depict his own projections, but also that he was connected with mind and spirit in a way that set him apart from his animal ancestors.

As we started to return to the earth's surface, the electric lights failed and we were left in total darkness until the guide found and lit a torch. In the darkness I felt strange forces, and in the torchlight I saw the paintings as Lascaux Man had seen them. I felt that I became a participant in the prehistoric ritual, overpowered by the beautiful paintings. I understood in a new way what Jung called the collective unconscious as a world of archetypal images.

I wrote to Dr. Jung and thanked him for his suggestion that led me to my profound experience of Lascaux. I also asked him if he would give me a final criticism on my book, for I felt he had not been critical enough.

On my return to Big Sur, I found a letter from Jung and took it out on the veranda to read.

Küsnacht, Zürich
October 3, 1957

Dear Miss Oakes,

Since you want to hear my opinion about your essay on the stone, I should say that I find it a bit too intellectual inasmuch as it considers the thought-images only, but as I have already called your attention to its *ambiente*, I miss the all-important feeling tone of the phenomenon. This is of exclusively artistic consideration, but if you want to do justice to the stone, you have to pay particular attention to the way, in which it is embedded in its surroundings: the water, the hills, the view, the peculiar atmosphere of the buildings, the nights and days, the seasons, sun, wind and rain and man living close to the earth, and yet remaining conscious in daily meditation of everything being just so. The air round the stone is filled with harmonies and disharmonies, with memories of times long ago, of vistas into the dim future with reverberations of a world far away, yet the so-called real world, into which the stone has fallen out of nowhere. A strange revelation and admonition. Try and dwell in this wholeness for a while and see what happens to you.

Sincerely yours,
C. G. Jung

I knew that I could never dwell in the wholeness of Bollingen, but I could and did dwell in my own Big Sur surroundings. With joy and contentment I gazed on my familiar landscape, the superb views from my house and my garden, situated more than a thousand feet above the Pacific Ocean. This circular view commands the four principle directions. To the south and west stretch the precipitous, serpentlike coastlines, and beyond this the sea wherein the sun sets. From this ocean, undulating hills and deep penetrating redwood canyons mount to east and north. These hills grow into heavily wooded mountains from behind which the sun rises. As I write this, the hills are burnt the color of honey, but with the winter rains they will become many shades of green.

Big Sur is still a wild country, and the earth gives forth an archetypal force that some people find too overpowering. The natives say: "The earth of Big Sur either accepts or rejects you." To my neighbors and me this force is creative and healing. Like Bollingen, Big Sur also has its "*genii loci.*" They are known as the mischievous "little green men," and they resemble the central figure on Jung's Stone. No wonder I found him friendly when I first saw him at Bollingen.

As at Bollingen, the Big Sur scenery is ever-changing, and one is conscious of the opposites always at work. Our wild winter storms uproot trees, blow off roof tops, and create massive landslides that block the highways. After the rains come crystal clear days that bring to the fore the distant landscape. These are days of pure sun and motionless sea. However, I love the days of the dense fog that swallows up the land and envelops my house. I feel contained, as though wrapped in something that feels like cotton wool. This ever-changing landscape is a constant marvel to me. It fills me with awe and deep humility. I give thanks that I can experience all this and that Big Sur is my home.

After rereading Jung's letter many times, I suddenly realized that in spite of all my research, it was not possible for me to interpret the Stone's meaning for its creator, Carl Jung, in his unique setting at Bollingen. I knew that I must put away all my notes and books and rid myself of my preconceived ideas. This emptying would open the way to what the Stone had to say directly to me at Big Sur—perhaps leading to an inner experience of healing and growing into wholeness. Now I knew what was to be my next important task.

CHAPTER
III

Stones

What we call the beginning is often the end
And to make an end is to make a beginning.
The end is where we start from. . . .
Every phrase and every sentence is an end and a beginning,
Every poem an epitaph. And any action
Is a step to the block, to the fire, down the sea's throat
Or to an illegible stone: and that is where we start.[1]

All my life I have collected stones of all sizes, shapes, and colors. Whether they were stones to gaze upon or to fondle, they all seemed to give me something of their mana. No wonder the path to my house in Big Sur is a series of pebble-mosaic steppingstones. Each steppingstone is a different symbol that I have made of colored pebbles from the sea. The last four steppingstones depict life symbols of progression, so that when one arrives at my door, one has more than arrived, for one then stands on a symbol of Tao. When my guest leaves the house, he or she symbolically regresses, since the symbols are reversed. When my friend Alan Watts saw this, he said, "When I depart I shall leave by the back door."

The Mam Indians with whom I lived in Guatemala feel that every stone contains a spirit. On the summit of one of their holy mountains, the shamans and prayer-makers worship a sacred stone in the form of a bird. It stands on an altar that I visited, and is surrounded by the remains of *copal* (incense), candles, and offerings. This did not seem strange to me, for throughout the ages man has worshipped rocks and stones as images of gods. No wonder I had felt so drawn to Jung's Stone in his garden at Bollingen.

With the photograph of the Stone in front of me on my desk, I began again the long, slow process of trying to grasp its inner meaning. The fact that I could feel the power of the carvings, and yet not really understand them, presented me with a challenge not only to my natural curiosity, but to all my acquired learning as well. More importantly, it was a challenge to something that lay hidden in me. In a way, it was the same kind of challenge that had led me to Peru and, before that, to live and work among the Indians of New Mexico and Guatemala.[2] I realized that my life with these so-called primitives who were one with nature—hence related to their own innermost being—had forced me to live with the two sides of my own nature before the Indians would accept me as someone they could trust. Unfortunately, I had lost the gift of contact with my inner self soon after I had returned to so-called civilization.

Closing my eyes, I pictured the Stone. It seemed to turn into the genuine Bollingen stone, Jung's Stone. I sensed its texture and even its pulse—for to me every object, animate or inanimate, has its own beat. Jung had said, ". . . every concrete object is always unknown in certain respects because we cannot know the ultimate nature of matter itself."[3]

In a trance, I laid my head against its hard, cold surface and asked the spirit of the Stone to give me of its mana. The Stone sank down, down within me, rather like a sinker on a fishing line. "If I attach a hook to the line, what can I use as bait?" I asked myself. "The carvings are the bait," a voice seemed to say. "They are the necessary enticement for you to experience the Stone's symbols in your own depths." This reminded me of the philosophy of Lao Tzu, who had said: "Possess the Uncarved Block and the world will yield to you of its own accord."[4] To Lao Tzu the Uncarved Block is a symbol of our own original nature; I must return to my "original nature" by the way of the carved Stone.

If in the course of the day's work the enigmatic text and symbols did not speak to me, I would question myself at bedtime before falling asleep. On awakening, I often received an answer in the form of a thought or dream. For years I had kept a record of my dreams and even illustrated them, trying to understand what they were telling me. Jung said:

The dream is a little hidden door in the innermost and most secret recesses of the soul, opening into that cosmic night which was psyche long before there was any ego-consciousness, and which will remain psyche no matter how far our ego-consciousness extends.[5]

Sometimes my mind was so occupied with the useless everyday thoughts that filled it that I could not go into the Stone nor could the Stone come into me. Like Jacob, I might have used the Stone as a pillow, and in my sleep the angels of heaven would have descended their ladder to enlighten me. Or should I have rubbed the Stone's hard surface until the genie of the Stone revealed himself and granted my wish?

Because of my many years of interest in symbolism, I could have made many guesses as to the readily accessible significance of the carved images. Yet I knew this was not the way to approach it. I felt I must try to remain open enough to receive what the Stone had to give, and then allow things to happen. The more I allowed things to happen without forcing them, without conscious intellectual effort, the more I began to realize that the images that came corresponded to some of Jung's deepest concepts.

Mandalas are now a familiar pattern to me. I began to understand their deep significance only when I read Jung's explanation of a mandala and saw the examples he had given. The word mandala is Sanskrit. It means circle or magic circle, and its symbolic representations have been found in all parts of the world from paleolithic times up to the present day. Mandalas are similar in design. The center, the most important part, is usually occupied by an image or symbol, like the child of the Stone. Arrayed about the central point are circles, squares, or triangles, and sometimes labyrinths.

Mandalas all give a feeling of order, harmony, and completion. I recall many examples of these designs: those painted on silk from China and Tibet, the rose windows of cathedrals of the Middle Ages, the frescoed domes of Byzantine churches, the inlaid floors of the round baptisteries of Italy, those in textiles and heraldry, and on pottery and ancient seals. One of the most familiar to me was the Mexican Aztec Calendar Stone. There are similar mandala designs in the codices of the Mayans, as well as in the carvings on their temples. They are found in sand paintings of the Navaho Indians, and in some modern paintings and drawings. They are not always found in pictorial form, but may appear in religious dances and ceremonies, in architecture, and even in literature. Music, too, often expresses a mandala form, as in Bach fugues or certain movements in symphonies.

In New Mexico I have seen Navaho medicine men heal patients with mandala-form sand paintings, in the same way that Jung's Stone healed me. Sickness in mind or body is driven out of the patient through his identification with the god depicted in the painting. At the moment of healing or transformation, the patient becomes the god; hence no evil or sickness can remain in the body. In the Far East, mandalas are used for meditation, healing, and transformation of the initiate's consciousness into a higher consciousness. "To a mind that is 'still' the whole universe surrenders."[6]

The alchemist of the Middle Ages made such designs. Some of them illustrated the steps in alchemy, which aimed to transmute matter into spirit, to find the alchemist's gold, or the philosophers' stone, the "Stone of the Wise." In analysis, mandala dreams or fantasies are also of a healing and transforming nature and are experienced in different forms appropriate to each stage of development. The analysand may eventually discover and experience his own mandala, "an inner representation of the soul."[7] This was not difficult for me to imagine, for I could see and feel the hypnotic power that came to me from Jung's mandala.

The mandala face of the Stone seemed to turn into a map, and the carvings became ways and means of finding the way into the psyche. Even though it was Jung's map, I felt that it was universal enough to become mine. The symbols were clues pointing the way to a treasure that lay deeply hidden within me. I felt that to understand the workings of the psyche, one has to feel like an explorer discovering a new world.

I compare Jung's explorations and discoveries to those of an archeologist, one who finds an ancient temple overgrown by a vast and unknown jungle. Over a period of many years, perhaps a lifetime, the obliterating jungle is cleared away, and the temple is seen to be a small part of a large city. The city unfolds its intricate plan as the vegetation is removed little by little. Then, with the screening of the soil and the cutting of many exploratory trenches that allow a view of what lies beneath the city, ever deeper and deeper layers of civilization are found, one on top of the other. During all this time, with the use of a scientific eye and profound comparative knowledge, the archeologist tabulates and fits together his findings like a puzzle, forming definite patterns.

In this way Jung, over a period of many years throughout almost the whole of his lifetime, probed and uncovered the layers of the human psyche and, as deeply as he probed, he found that it is fathomless. He said: "Our psyche is part of nature, and its enigma is as limitless. Thus we cannot define either the psyche or nature. We can merely state what we believe them to be and describe, as best we can, how they function."[8]

Jung says in his memoirs:

If the human [soul] is anything, it must be of unimaginable complexity and diversity, so that it cannot possibly be approached through a mere psychology of instinct. I can only gaze with wonder and awe at the depths and heights of our psychic nature. Its non-spatial universe conceals an untold abundance of images which have accumulated over millions of years of living development and become fixed in the organism. My consciousness is like an eye that penetrates to the most distant spaces, yet it is the psychic non-ego that fills them with nonspatial images. And these images are not pale shadows, but tremendously powerful psychic factors. . . . Beside this picture I would like to place the spectacle of the starry heavens at night, for the only equivalent of the universe within is the universe without; and just as I reach this world through the medium of the body, so I reach that world through the medium of the psyche.[9]

So I looked on the Stone as a symbol of a human psyche. I saw the carvings as clues or ways leading into a new world, into a psyche itself, a fearful, fascinating land full of mystery.

The Way is like an empty vessel
That yet may be drawn from
Without ever needing to be filled.
It is bottomless; the very progenitor of all things in the world.
In it all sharpness is blunted,
All tangles untied,
All dust smoothed.
It is like a deep pool that never dries.
Was it too the child of something else? We cannot tell.
But as a substanceless image it existed before the Ancestor.[10]

Through these layers of the psyche Jung charted an inner course, a psychological way. He named it the "individuation process," a process of consciously coming to terms with one's "inner center" and becoming a complete individual. This concept is based on his scientific observations of the human psyche and his profound knowledge of comparative mythology, alchemy, and comparative religion. As a boat must have a pilot to conduct it through uncharted waters to port, so must the average person have a guide to take him by the hand, step by step, helping him consciously to experience the dark unexplored waters of the unconscious, to approach the inner center of his being.

It seemed perfectly natural to me that Jung's Stone mandala should be an Opener of the Door and that the little figure in the center—his discovered treasure, the end of his treasure hunt—should represent my inner journey's beginning. I looked on Jung's Stone as a ritual instrument and the child figure as a sort of guide to help me find my own mandala and its center, the treasure.

If the treasure already has been found, does it mean that I am starting at the end? But what is end and what is beginning? Where does the beginning begin and where does the end end? Again, I think of Eliot:

> . . . In order to arrive there,
> To arrive where you are, to get from where you are not,
>   You must go by a way wherein there is no ecstasy.
> In order to arrive at what you do not know
>   You must go by a way which is the way of ignorance.
> In order to possess what you do not possess
>   You must go by the way of dispossession.
> In order to arrive at what you are not
>   You must go through the way in which you are not.
> And what you do not know is the only thing you know
> And what you own is what you do not own,
> And where you are is where you are not.[11]

The poem ends with "In my end is my beginning."

As I looked at the figure, the child standing in its circle, it seemed to invite me within. Must I go down into the circle to come up and out again? Would this mean I would be looking at the Stone from the outside in? And once I went down, like Alice into the rabbit hole, would I view the Stone from the inside out?

Jung's child was indeed inviting me to go within, to turn back to my own beginnings, to meet and know the child or babe that was within me.

Looking again at the two circles on the Stone, I asked myself, "What is a circle?" A circle is round, without beginning or end; it is complete and stands for wholeness or totality. This reminded me of a dream that Jung told to a friend: ". . . he saw a huge round block of stone sitting on a high plateau and at the foot of the stone were engraved these words: 'And this shall be a sign unto you of wholeness and Oneness'."[12] I was also reminded of the uroborus, the gnostic circular serpent with its tail in its mouth, that symbolizes eternity and is considered to be complete within itself.

The circle is also a symbol of protection, the magic circle, the pass-me-not. What about my world, my spinning circular world, and the mysterious cosmos that surrounds it, a universe of order and harmony, in contrast to my world of chaos, a large circle encircling another, like the two circles on the Stone? I also thought of my two personal worlds, visible and invisible. I could scarcely compare the confused visible world I lived in to the cosmos. Could I compare my unconscious, my little-known world, to the order and harmony of the cosmos?

To answer these questions I sought to control my mind, to keep it from wandering around in circles, and to take the next step forward to try to find order and wholeness within myself.

CHAPTER
IV

The Search

Like many members of the younger generation of the '60s, I too had searched many years for a way of life different from the social one into which I had been born. Unfortunately, I was not clearly aware of what I was seeking, for I kept looking for the answer in people to whom I was especially drawn—a lover, a teacher of Yoga or Zen, or some other kind of Master. Since I never found what I was seeking, these experiences were always disillusioning, especially when I would discover that the teacher's personal life did not coincide with what he taught.

A number of years passed before I realized that I had a mother problem, and decided to put myself into the hands of a Jungian psychotherapist recommended by a close friend for whom I had great respect. This turned into a deeply traumatic experience, for the therapist had not had adequate training—and in a way I blamed this partly on Jung himself, since I felt he had not taken steps to prevent unqualified people from practicing in his name. After I had worked for many months with the therapist, the day came when my unconscious rescued me from our mutual negative transference. I was sitting in the chair opposite her when I saw to my horror that the walls of the room were closing in on me. In panic I jumped to my feet. "I am leaving you," I cried, "and I will not return."

The therapist, too, got up, and in an emotional voice replied: "You are so much liver on a board—so much sewer down the drain. You are on the edge of a volcano, and if you leave me you will fall in." I was shocked numb at what I heard. My voice re-

35

turned as I opened the door. Facing the therapist, who had now become for me the essence of evil, I said, "Better to fall in."

It took me more than a year to recover from that devastating experience. I often walked the city streets in despair, trying to comprehend my inner turmoil. Looking up at the many night-lit windows of hotels and apartment houses that I passed, I imagined tragic and unhappy dramas going on behind them. Strangely enough, this always made me feel more cheerful about my own situation. To try to get away from it all, I went to Europe and rented a cottage with two friends in a fishing village in the south of France, where my cousin Jerome was living.

I kept to myself my inner turmoil, which was still with me. At times I felt so upset that I wondered whether I would crack. During the day I was kept busy with my friends and my cousin, painting, cooking, and swimming. But at night, I often prayed for help. Finally help came to me, although not at all in the way I had expected. At the time I did not understand fully the mystery of my animal visitors. I can see now, however, that the healing help I needed came to me at the instinctual animal stratum of my psyche.

A few weeks after our arrival in France, as I sat in the sun on the terrace, I saw a small white terrier at the entrance gate. The little dog walked right in. Ignoring everybody else, it immediately adopted me, and I, it. For a short while the dog gave me just what I craved, affection and understanding at an animal level.

One day, however, it moved on, and I felt a great loss until its place was filled by a visiting cat, which also adopted me. After a month the cat left, and I wondered what magic would happen next. Several nights later, I had a very vivid dream of a turtle that had become my friend. At breakfast I told my companions of the dream, which was still with me. After breakfast I walked in the grass to the back of the house, and cried out in amazement when I came upon a good-sized turtle. I then remembered a Chinese painting of a turtle supporting the world on its back, and I wondered if this turtle had come to hold up my tottering world. I had never heard of the word synchronicity, so I did not realize what a synchronous event this was, although I did know that it was a rare occurrence, since turtles were not common in this village. From then on, I was more partial to turtles than to psychotherapists.

A year or so later I decided to move to Paris and become an artist. Before leaving America for France, I naively made up my mind to sever myself from my puritanical upbringing and to experience everything. That, I thought, would be really living. But since I was unrelated to the unknown side of myself, my search for something—I knew not what—led me always into outer experiences of a disillusioning nature. I still felt erroneously that whatever it was that I was searching for lay in the other person.

Although I had many friends, both men and women, my relation to women was always difficult because of my unconscious mother problem. For several years I had been aware that I was disturbed by being too close to women. This made me wonder whether I had a bisexual nature, or whether, unconsciously, I felt my women friends were mother figures. I remember my mother once saying: "Anyone who has a physical relationship to their own sex should be locked up in an insane asylum." As I have an inquisitive nature, this remark did not deter me from experimentation.

So, to find out for myself, I had a few affairs, not only with men but also with a woman. Unfortunately, all these people were not only as unconscious as I was, but also as inexperienced as I in the art of love and sexual expression. My chief fault was that I entered into these experiences without real feeling, expecting to find within my partner the answer for which I was searching. My fear of catching a venereal disease or becoming pregnant, as well as a deep, unconscious fear of being possessed, did not help at all. From then on, I knew I did not want to belong to anyone. Marriage was not for me.

From the point of view of my mother and her friends, this seemed a failure. From my own viewpoint, however, I now see that it was a virtue. I had already developed along the lines of singleness of purpose, and although later on I had a series of experiences that almost ended in marriage, I could never take the final step before asking myself, and thinking over carefully, a certain question. As breakfast is a very important meal to me, almost a religious ceremony, I devised a fantasy that infallibly helped me to make a decision. I would visualize the man in question sitting opposite me at a small round table, sharing my sacred breakfast. "Do I want to have breakfast with him every morning for the rest of my life?" I would ask myself, and the answer was always, "No."

In the years that followed my disastrous first encounter with analysis, I read some of Jung's books with great interest, but it was not until I met Jung and saw his Stone at Bollingen in 1951 that the thought of having a real analysis entered my mind. I was by then more than aware that to experience and understand consciously the inscriptions and symbols of the Stone, I must first of all know myself; hence I decided I should engage again in analysis. Apparently Jung knew this when he suggested two years later that his analyst friend Dr. L. serve as a consultant about the Stone. I had already heard a great deal about Dr. L., but had never met him.

One night, however, I dreamt of him, and the dream remained with me all the next day. Interpreting this dream as an Opener of the Door, I made an appointment with Dr. L., not for an analysis, but just to satisfy my curiosity. From the many dreams I had collected over the year, I chose one to take to him that I could neither understand nor forget. It had to do with my mother's liver. I learned later that it clearly presented to Dr. L. my whole mother problem and the trauma I had suffered years before from the first psychotherapist.

I liked Dr. L. instantly, and found him sympathetic, understanding, intelligent, handsome, and rather like a shaman. I noticed that he had in his office one of the books I had written, and an illustration from it in his waiting room. But although this pleased me, I decided not to commit myself. I did not want to put my soul yet in anyone's hands, even those of a doctor suggested by C. G. Jung.

Several months later, Dr. L. telephoned me to say he was in nearby Carmel. He had seen Jung in Switzerland, and had been told about the proposed film on Jung and my research on the Stone. Jung had asked Dr. L., if he were ever near Big Sur and it were convenient, to call on me to see how the work for Jerome's film was progressing. I invited the doctor and his charming wife for luncheon, and afterwards showed him my research material on the Stone. It was developing into a book about which Jung did not yet know. I also showed him some paintings of my dreams that I had made over the years.

By the time he left I knew he was going to have to be my analyst, so I wrote him a letter asking if he would be my guide in the inner world. After a few days, I went to San Francisco to

commence my journey into the unknown land of my own unconscious.

Not only did I enter a new world, but I had to learn a new
language—a psychological one, with its difficult, stilted vocabu-
lary, words that Jungians use to describe the processes of the
psyche, such as *personal unconscious, collective unconscious,
persona, the shadow, anima* and *animus, archetypes, complexes,
libido, the Self, the opposites, the four functions of consciousness,
the transcendental function,* and many others. I knew their surface meanings from Jung's books, but only by experiencing these
words in my analysis did I learn what they might truly convey to
me.

I learned that, symbolically, the unconscious is often pictured
as an ocean or any body of water. In mythology the hero or hero-
ine has to descend into the watery depths or into the womb of
the earth to bring back the treasure that lies there. In nature,
trees and plants have to send their roots down into the earth,
drawing the necessary moisture that enables them to grow upward and outward and so produce their flowers and fruits and
reproduce themselves.

The alchemists of the Middle Ages who were so important to
Jung also felt that from the lowly came the highest, that from the
earth or water in their retorts could come gold, even the Philosophers' Stone. We are born out of the maternal fluid of the womb
and out of the living waters of the unconscious. Speaking of his
theory regarding the primary source of life energy, Dr. Szent-
Gyorgi, one of the world's foremost biochemists, says: "The body's
water ceases to be just a neutral medium and becomes part of
the living material, part of the living machine, part of the basic
life process."[1]

Water, what do I feel about water? On the Stone I found the
dark watery elements of the unconscious symbolized by the dark
waning moon. Deep, dark water has always held the fear of the
unknown for me; just as I avoid finding myself in deep waters, so
have I ignored the dark side of my nature. I never knew what
creature lurking in the depths might reach out and pull me under or what tidal wave might arise and engulf and drown me. But
there is another kind of water: heavenly water, living water, pure
water, distilled water; ice, snow, snow crystals full of beauty and
mystery. Rain, rainwater that the world prays for, rain for the

crops, rain to purify our bodies, water from the well, baptismal water—the water of becoming, the water that heals and from which comes birth and rebirth.

The Taoists believed that from the low came the high, that "Tao, like water 'takes the low ground,'" and that the low ground is the "dwelling-place of Tao."[2]

Meditating on the Stone, I saw the large circle turn into a sphere similar to the globe of the world that I remember from my childhood classrooms. This sphere must symbolize the conscious aspect of my psyche—my world. Its hidden interior was unconscious. Within this unconscious are two layers of depth, according to Jung, the personal and the collective unconscious. The personal unconscious lies closest to the surface, in the space between the two circles, or between the core and the outer surface of the sphere. The collective unconscious, on the other hand, is the fathomless core of the globe, the inner circle within which the child Mercury stands. And these two circles, the inner and the outer, remind me now of the experience I had later under the influence of LSD.

On that occasion, after I had closed my eyes, severing myself from my world of the senses, I seemed to descend, down, down, into a fearful, round, fathomless black well. On my way down I vaguely saw several strata of tunnels, like rabbit warrens leading off horizontally from my vertical descent. After a seemingly endless journey I arrived at the bottom—another world made up of impenetrable blackness, a darkness in which time did not exist. But far off in the distance I saw a speck of light. Groping my way toward it, I finally arrived at an opening leading out of the darkness into the light. To the left of this opening I perceived a vague outline of an enormous serpent coiled into a figure eight. I could not distinguish its head nor tail, but passed by without fear, for it was not threatening. Then I returned to my conscious world by ascending the way I had descended.

I see the unconscious as an artesian well. To dig this well, I would have to penetrate with great difficulty an outer stratum of rocky, sandy soil, a layer that symbolizes all the personal memories that would be forgotten or repressed. Beneath it, there would lie an immeasurable depth represented by a stratum of rock. I would have to tap through this rock to release the reserve of water that would then flow spontaneously from inner pressure. I see that water as the collective unconscious. I found these same divisions on the carved Stone.

The reserve of water that flows spontaneously from inner pressure is the collective psychic material that we have inherited. It is part of every human being. We are born with it; it remains part of our make-up. It existed before we became conscious and before our personalities were formed; as we know, the conscious is born out of the unconscious. How can I question the fact that the basic processes of the psyche are the same in all people, or that the symbols that express these processes are similar, any more than I can question the similarity of man's physical make-up?

Jung says:

> As the evolution of the embryonic body repeats its prehistory, so the mind also develops through a series of prehistoric stages. The main task of dreams is to bring back a sort of 'recollection' of the prehistoric, as well as the infantile world, right down to the level of the most primitive instincts.[3]

> What we properly call instincts are physiological urges, and are perceived by the senses. But at the same time, they also manifest themselves in fantasies and often reveal their presence only by symbolic images. These manifestations are what I call the archetypes.[4]

To illustrate an archetype, Jung told Jerome and me the following story, which I later learned appears in his essay on synchronicity:

> When one is in an archetypal situation, things happen in a strange way. A patient I had once was a very well brought up French girl, with a very ordered brain, a typical product of French education. It was hard for her to upset this, to get under it. It was impossible for me to reach beyond it. We had worked together for over a year; I had been unable to reach her. One day she came to me with a dream she had had. We were sitting near a closed window which gave on the garden. She had dreamed that someone had brought her from Egypt a present of a golden scarab, a symbol of the rising sun, of happiness, of realization, of all sorts of good things. The scarab is an archetype. As she told me her dream, I heard a fluttering on the window pane. I opened the window and took what was there in my hand and saw it was a beetle. It was of emerald green and

golden color, you know, the beetles that we have here, almost like scarabs. She did not see it until I opened my hand and placed it on her knee. She almost fainted. From then on she was able to communicate with me and I with her. It is unwise to feel that there is any causality here, that one thing happened because of another. Rather, all of these things happened because of the same primal cause. The scarab's need of her and her need of the scarab were the same thing. All of nature is in our patterns; we are not separate.

Again meditating on the Stone, picturing the three vibrating zig-zag lines and the undulating line that join the inner and outer circles, I saw that their seemingly electric movement is inward and outward and backward and forward, the same kind of movement that Jung attributed to psychic energy and the Taoists to Tao. Jung thought of this energy as "a psychic analogue of physical energy."[5] The zig-zag lines gave the sensation of expansion and contraction, like the tides of the sea that move from the center of the ocean mass, the inner world, to the shores of the land masses, the outer world. Like the ocean, psychic energy is always in motion; according to Jung, the motion comes from the tension of opposites.[6] When I think of opposites in relation to energy, the negative and positive poles of an electric battery come to mind. Analogously, I know that the two poles of my psyche are the conscious and unconscious sides of my nature. To relieve their tension within me, I have to look at the contents from the unconscious deep that come to the surface in dreams and projections, and try to understand them. This leads to an experience of both sides of myself, and the bringing together of the opposites.

When I look back on my childhood, I realize that most of my training and education were suited for a sensory or outer world existence only. My inner world was almost completely neglected. Dreams and fantasies were laughed at or taboo, and consequently were associated with the unknown, the night, fear, and evil. My questions about God were never satisfactorily answered, so I wondered if He, like Santa Claus, was an invention of my elders. I believed in fairies, and I shared this secret with chosen playmates. But fear of the night and of my dream world persisted until I learned that my dreams and the night were not sources of evil and therefore were not to be feared.

I never thought of the opposites that were all around me until I was in analysis. How did I know that black was black unless I was aware of white? In observing nature I was often overwhelmed by such breathtaking beauty that at the moment of feeling this intense pleasure, I felt sharp pain. How similar this is to being in love—moments of supreme joy may simultaneously be moments of the deepest sadness. The opposites cannot be separated. We cannot pry apart the conscious side of our psyche and the unconscious, any more than we can separate the sunny side of a stone from the shady side. But we can recognize the two sides of the stone as one stone.

The Chinese symbol of the Great Monad also pictures two divisions, duality which is one—like the two sides of man's nature. The white side was called Yang and was considered by the Chinese to be male, active, positive, and associated with the sun. Yin was black and, in contrast to Yang, was female, passive, negative, and associated with the moon. These two divisions were ". . . interdependent and complementary facets of existence, and the aim of *yin-yang* philosophers was . . . the attainment in human life of perfect balance between the two principles."[7]

Throughout my analysis I had many dreams of the opposites. A common dream was of passing a barrier from one country to another, as in my initial dream. I remember a later dream of planting a seed between dry sandy soil and rich fertile soil. This was obviously an attempt to bring the two worlds together. All of this suggested to me that if I could experience, recognize, and accept what arose from the unconscious, I would bring the two sides of myself together and achieve a feeling of stability and of wholeness.

While I was engrossed in thinking of the opposites, a voice seemed to say to me: "Look at me in the center of Jung's Stone. I stand between the opposites. As the center of this mandala I am between the four radiating lines of energy. I am between the Moon and the Sun and Jupiter and Venus; Mars is beneath my feet and Saturn is above my head."

Gazing on the Stone, I wondered whether it could be the child Mercury who had spoken to me, so I questioned him: "As the point between the opposites, are you the energy that can synthesize these opposites within your own nature?"

He did not answer. Instead, I thought of a saying of Jung's: "Every step forward, even the smallest, along the path of consciousness, adds to the world, to the visible and tangible God. There is no consciousness without the distinguishing of opposites."[8]

Picturing the mandala face of the Stone, I visualized again the large circle framed by the earth square, and the radiating lines that extended toward the corners of the square. Mercury must have waved his magic wand, for the large circle became a compass and the four lines were pointing to the four principle directions in space. Looking on this compass, as if it functioned in my own inner and outer worlds, I saw the Child-Spirit as the needle of the compass magnetized by the earth, pointing out directions in my psyche. Its four directions I compared to Jung's four functions of consciousness: thinking, feeling, sensation, and intuition, "the four 'modes of apprehension' by which the ego takes in and assimilates the material coming from without and within."[9] An extrovert like myself has a compass only in the outer world. An introvert has one in his or her special world, the inner world. The challenge is to develop a compass that will function in both worlds.

Of the four functions within each person, one is always much more conscious and favored than the others, and that one is called the "superior or dominant function." Its direct opposite, the "inferior function," is usually buried deeply in the unconscious; the other two functions are then semiconscious. Jung found that feeling and thinking are opposites, and he called them *rational functions*. Intuition and sensation similarly are opposites, and he called them *irrational functions*.

My dominant function, I learned, is sensation; accordingly, my inferior function is intuition, that inner function that apprehends directly what is in the future or what arises from within. My secondary function is feeling, and I now understand what "feeling" signifies. It is not emotion. It evaluates a situation or an experience by feeling into it. I was the sort of person who would say, "No! That is not right," or, "This is wonderful!" with no basis but feeling for my judgment.

Thinking is my third function, and I am now trying to cultivate it. When I was in analysis, I noticed that I always seemed to make new friends with thinking-intuitive people—my opposites. Consequently, it was a real challenge to continue seeing these friends, for I could never fully understand them. By trying to comprehend them I became more aware of my own thinking and intuitive functions. Jung was a thinking-intuitive type, so his opposite functions must originally have been feeling-sensation. Maybe the gods on the Stone symbolized, in his world, the four functions that he had learned through the years to integrate from the unconscious into his conscious ego world. I felt that maybe, now, they would help me to accomplish the same sort of integration.

CHAPTER
V

Creation

In almost all myths of Creation, first there was nothingness. It was usually pictured as a vast abyss of dark water, soundless and without motion, yet containing the potentiality of all creation. Out of this evolved an energy—the desire to create. It came into existence out of nonexistence. It divided itself by a light, a breath, a thought, or a word. It became multiple, "the one became many."

My favorite creation myth comes from the Mayans:

This is the account of how all was in suspense, all calm, in silence: all motionless, still, and the expanse of the sky was empty. . . . The surface of the earth had not yet appeared, there was only the calm sea and the great expanse of the sky. There was nothing brought together, nothing which could make a noise, not anything which might move, or tremble, or could make a noise in the sky. There was nothing standing: only the calm water, the placid sea, alone and tranquil. . . . Nothing existed, there was only immobility and silence in the darkness, in the night. Only the creator, the Maker, Tepeu, Gacumatz [The Great Mother, the Great Father] were in the water surrounded with light. They were hidden under green and blue feathers. . . . By nature they were great sages and thinkers. In this manner the sky existed and also the heart of Heaven, which is the name of God and thus he is called. Then came the word, Tepeu and Gucamatz came together in the darkness [the Great Cosmic Serpent], in the night. . . . They talked then, discussing and deliberating: they agreed, they united their words and their thoughts [the coming of consciousness]. Then while they meditated it be-

47

came clear to them that when dawn would break, man must appear. Then they planned the creation, and the growth of trees and the thickets and the birth of life and the creation of man. Thus it was arranged in the darkness and in the night by the Heart of Heaven who is called Huracan.[1]

Very similar to an ancient creating myth is the division of a sex cell. When the spiral-shaped sperm cell with its male and female chromosomes penetrates the female egg, it is like the snake-line of the Stone entering the inner circle in which Mercury stands; it is similar also to the line that divides the Yang and Yin of the Taoists. The chromosomes of these two cells unite, and man and woman mingle the halves of their structures and character, like the Yang and Yin. From this union the egg-sperm cell divides from two to four and thence to the many. "The union of the sun and moon gives birth to the stars. . . ."

Thinking about creation myths, I shut my eyes and clearly saw the mandala face of the Stone. I had an intense feeling that something might happen. Perhaps the child Mercury would struggle out of its protective circle, like a babe out of its mother's womb. From the mysterious unconscious it would be born into consciousness. I thought of my own birth and remembered what my mother had told me about it. She said that I had nearly died shortly after birth because of enormous hives that had spread over my body and inside my throat, causing it almost to close. As soon as I was put on a formula, I recovered. This certainly showed a potent allergy to my mother's milk.

I have remarkably clear childhood memories of my father and of my brother, who was three years older, since they were both very close to me. We seemed to understand one another. My relations to my sister and mother, however, were exceedingly vague. I remember absolutely nothing about my sister, who was eight years older than I, until I reached puberty; I remember only two episodes connected with my mother.

The first memory is of the time my father took me to see my mother sitting behind a closed window. She had diphtheria, and we all had to have preventive shots, which terrified me. I probably associated the fear with my mother, and therefore unconsciously blamed her. The second memory concerns the day of my father's death. I was only seven-and-a-half, and had been kept in the country with my nurse and my brother. Early that morning, I dreamt that I saw my father walking out the front door of our town house. He waved to me and said good-by as he vanished upward. Waking my nurse, I told her the dream. Afterwards she checked the time of my father's death and found that it was approximately at the time of my dream.

Later in the day we were taken back to the city house, and I clearly remember my mother dressed all in black with just a touch of white at her throat. She was seated at the end of our oval dining room table; I stood at the other end. She motioned me to come to her. I put my hands behind my back and refused to budge. We just gazed at each other. How I must have hurt her, for unconsciously I must have blamed her for my father's death, since he had understood me and I loved him.

My mother was a wonderful woman. She had great dignity and inner beauty and was admired and loved by those who knew her. But there was very little affection between us; she was so introverted that she was unable to express her feelings. I have no memory of her holding me close or kissing me with warmth, so I remained withdrawn and closed toward her.

When I was about ten years old, we left the West, where I had been born, and moved to New York, where my mother had lived before her marriage. I was put in a private day school for young ladies. I felt like an uprooted weed planted in a hothouse. I had no persona, and was the first Westerner in the school. The sophisticated girls looked at me with great curiosity, and one even asked me if I had lived in a teepee. I must have had some ego, for I solved my feelings of inferiority in several ways. I would say to myself, "What a bunch of snobs they are! Westerners are far superior. These Easterners may know all about opera, concerts, boys, and clothes, but I bet they can't bridle and saddle a horse or light a campfire in the rain." If they told jokes I did not comprehend, I would laugh with them, pretending I understood. To call attention to myself, I broke rules and concentrated on sports instead of studies. Latin was not a favorite subject with me, so the day I was asked to conjugate *pigo* I stood up and said, "Pigo, pigire, squeelie, gruntum." I was dismissed from the class and sent home with a letter to my mother from the principal.

By comparison with my friends' relationships with their mothers, I realized that all was not as it should be between my mother and me. My dreams and the feeling of tension between us also told me this. Later there was not only tension but a deep chasm that opened up when I refused to attend holy communion. I had accepted the Episcopalian religion without thought, since it was a part of my family life. Not until I was in my teens, when I attended confirmation classes at St. Bartholomew on Park Avenue, did I begin to question what had been taught me. The minister's explanations of the ritual of confirmation seemed unreal and boring and held no spiritual value for me. When I knelt with the class at the altar rail for our first communion, I did what the others did, but symbolically I could not accept the bread and wine as the body and blood of Christ. From then on I refused to take communion, for I felt I would be acting a lie.

On Christian holidays like Christmas and Easter, I always went to church with my family but did not take communion. When they left me sitting alone in our pew to go to the altar, I felt lonely and estranged. My mother was very upset by my stand, for she was deeply religious. I know I must have hurt her deeply. At the time it seemed impossible for us to understand each other or to do anything about it, since we were both so unconscious of the real situation. However, in giving up communion I did not turn my back on God or Christ. I believed deeply within myself in a God, in a force or something beyond my comprehension. It was just the automatic way religion was presented to me that I could not accept.

I had my first religious experience when I was in my early twenties. I was in Java with my mother and two friends. We had just visited the extraordinary Buddhist stupa of Borobudur. I left the others, and entered the door of a nearby Buddhist temple alone. Stepping from the brilliant tropical light into the darkness of the temple was like walking from midday into midnight. As I stood quietly inside the door, I gradually discerned an immense Buddha that seemed to fill the whole temple. My eyes traveled from floor level upward; I bent my head way back to see the face of the Buddha, shrouded in mystery. How beautiful, how serene and how peaceful his face is, I thought. At that moment, a shock went through me like a bolt of lightning. My whole body tingled, and I felt deeply moved, knowing that God had visited me. From then on, my interest in eastern religious thought influenced me greatly.

I wanted very much to go to boarding school, but was forced

to live at home with my mother. Later I wanted to take a job, but felt guilty about having such thoughts, for then my mother would be left alone, since my sister had married and my brother lived in another city. Not until I finally left home and was independent did my mother and I begin to understand one another. Finally we were able to relate to each other, to express our feelings and to enjoy each other's company. Yet my feeling of guilt lingered, remaining with me until I had the following very important dream:

> I heard a doorbell ring. Before opening the door I put a chain on it, for I felt something evil was on the other side. I opened the door a crack and saw a short, squat, shapeless middle-aged woman. She was dreadful to look upon and I was pleased that I had put the chain on the door. This proved to be no barrier, for she glided through the door into the room. I took two carving knives that I found on the kitchen table and with one in each hand went after the horrible woman. I faced her in the hall and saw my own mother standing in back of her. The two knives turned into one curved sword that was shaped like a new moon. I ran it through the disgusting woman twice. It was terrifying, for I could feel her flesh.

I did not then understand this dream, but I felt it must be a warning of some kind, so I wrote it down in the dream book I had kept for many years. At the time of this dream I was working with Navaho medicine men. The purifying ceremony had been performed over me, and I had been given a new name.

Later, in analysis, I understood that the squat woman of the dream was the evil side of the engulfing universal Great Mother, similar to the waning black moon on Jung's Stone, and also to Hecate, the Greek goddess, mistress of the west gate of the underworld, the gate of death. She could pass through the door, for her power was magic, black magic. I went after this malevolent sorceress with two knives: two, a negative female number, and this turned into a sword, one, a positive male number in the shape of a new moon, a positive female symbol of rebirth. It would take the negative power of the number two, plus the positive power of the one and the new moon, a symbol of the soul, to do away with the devouring, corrupt, destructive mother. Dr. Jacobi wrote: "If the individual is to develop and consolidate his ego, the 'mother' as the symbol of the darkness of unconscious-

ness must first be destroyed by the bright light of youthful consciousness, symbolized by the sun's rays or by the arrow, *sword,*
or club."[2] My personal mother stood in back of the Great Mother,
showing that she was the one I must face next.

Wondering about my psyche and my birth, I asked myself:
What is my own creation myth? And a voice seemed to say: "Just
as consciousness is born from the unconscious, so were you
born out of the watery darkness of your mother's womb into the
light of day and your world of space, time, and form. This was
your first birth."

I thought I understood, but I knew that it would clarify my
thoughts to use symbols to illustrate parts of my personal myth.
To me symbols are often better than words, since they can be a
sort of shorthand about very complex unknown factors.

First I see a circle similar to the Chinese circle of emptiness,
the T'ai Chi. It seems empty and without motion and yet it holds
everything within it. It is beyond man's comprehension.

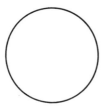 

I look again. The circle has become active. It has formed a
central nucleus, a spark, a seed which is eternal and latent in everything behind all creation. This symbol is similar to the Two of
Chinese philosophy. Lao Tzu says of it:

> There was something formless yet complete,
> That existed before heaven and earth;
> Without sound, without substance,
> Dependent on nothing, unchanging,
> All pervading, unfailing.
> One may think of it as the mother of all things under heaven.
> Its true name we do not know;
> "Way" [Tao] is the by-name that we give it.[3]

The circle's activity, which I feel as psychic energy, produces
another circle, an outer shell, a circle of physical energy. I look
on these two circles with their central nucleus, the Self, as sym-

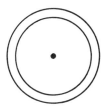

bolic of the mysterious human psyche, which is unknowable and potential. It symbolizes my psyche, as part of my mother's psyche before birth, and during the first year of life. I heard the voice again. "Between one and two years of age," it said, "the Self separates from the mother and becomes the center of the child's psyche."

I understood this as the commencement of separation. The outer circle, my outer personality, moving toward independence, away from the central nucleus, forming and separating my ego from the Self, yet still under the power of the Self.

The voice continued:

"Around the age of three your ego was born into consciousness and became the center of your conscious personality."

Yes, I thought, my outer personality with its ego center is a product of my original inner personality with its central psychic nucleus, the Self. Although they are two, they are felt as one insofar as I am aware of my psyche as a whole.[4]

The voice spoke on: "As your ego grew along with your expanding horizon, it should have developed enough strength by the time you reached puberty to enable you to face your mother, free yourself from her binding hold, and become a somewhat independent human being. You would then have been able to relate to her. However, this was quite impossible for you because of the early death of your father and your unconscious relationship with your mother. From puberty to your late twenties you began to feel that you were trapped in the society that you had been brought up in, and were tied to your mother by cords of guilt for which you unconsciously blamed her."

I could not but agree. However, since I had been the only one left at home, I had felt it my duty to remain with my mother. Though I went away on trips, sometimes for as long as a year, I never actually thought of leaving home until I was jolted into it by my mother's refusal, on one occasion, to allow me to invite a certain man friend home for dinner. "He is not a gentleman," she said. What she feared was that I might marry him, and not make the socially advantageous marriage she desired for me.

A second jolt was a restaurant scene I witnessed. A mother and daughter were dining at a table near mine, and the daughter looked older than the mother. Her sad, lost expression and her drained, dry, sexless body horrified me, and I knew that this must not happen to Maud Oakes.

"So it was not until you took the final step," the voice continued, "and left home, that you really began to experience life with all its problems and challenges, and to work them out." Then it added: "That was a pattern of ego growth that you should have commenced much earlier."

From the time I left home, I explored the esoteric side of life. Friends helped me, particularly one who became for a while a very much needed spiritual guide. She was a remarkable woman who had had an amazing life that she had profited by. She had an uncanny ability to sense the creative potentiality in other people. This spiritual journey of mine, which lasted seven years, opened vast new horizons and afforded me much needed training in the fields of mythology, symbolism, and theosophy. But those who helped me the most were the Indians. The six years or more that I spent with them while I was doing ethnological work was a very positive experience, since I was completely on my own and cut off from all the friends on whom previously I had been dependent.

My Navaho initiation, I realized, had been a preliminary step toward individuation, and it had happened because I had been searching for something new. I had felt disgusted with the useless life that I had been leading. It had been almost as if a spiritual force had taken hold of my destiny and opened the door a crack, so that I might step through into another world. More than ever, that had put me in touch with "the little voice within." From then on I knew that what I sought lay within me, and not in any other person. It was only then that my ego could become fully developed.

As I congratulated myself, the voice interrupted me, saying: "Yes, I agree. It was when you were living and working with the Indians that you came from this achievement of ego strength to the threshold leading to individuation, but it was not until you met me, carved on Dr. Jung's Stone, that you started your real journey into depth."

And indeed! It had been only when I had seen the Stone, its mandala face and its little hooded child-like daemon, that I had been touched to my depth and allowed it to hook me. "Yes, it was you, Hermes-Mercury," I said, "who put me in touch with the unconscious and analysis, you, Jung, and then Dr. L., and Dr. O., a woman analyst. What a long, difficult journey into the abyss of my psyche this has become! A spiritual journey into death for re-birth; death of the old Maud Oakes for a new."

I thought of what Dr. L. had one day said to me: "It is the task of the ego in the second half of life to redirect energy away from the physical world of the body towards the Self, and to do it consciously, so as to learn how to return to this central arche-type at the approach of death."

As the ego is really the outer manifestation or projection of the Self, I visualize my ego as now returning to its original source: the seed of my soul, the Self.

And this return, when accomplished, will symbolize the goal of my individuation: the ego, as the center of my outer world and the Self coming together; the pairs of opposites transformed into an image of "wholeness." The final "spiritual end" which has no end, and is like an empty circle that holds all within it.

CHAPTER VI

The Unknown World

In the beginning of my analysis with Dr. L., I looked on the unconscious as a rather frightening world. It was unknown to me, and I never knew what to expect. As I became more deeply involved, my dream world became my real world, and I felt I stood apart from friends and my old patterns of existence. This feeling was similar to the one I had when I first returned from Guatemala. It was as if there was a pane of glass between my friends and myself. I could see them, but I made no effort to hear them —we were in two different worlds. And in Big Sur I often had this feeling, especially when I left my work to go down to the highway to fetch my mail. My neighbors and I awaited the arrival of the mailman, and often I heard myself saying "yes" or "no" to a question to which I had not been listening. No wonder the hippies were trying one thing after another to discover an inner real world, a world of which they could feel a part, a spiritual world, different from the outward one of material values. According to Eastern philosophy, the material world is one of illusion.

Jung has said about dreams:

> A story told by the conscious mind has a beginning, a development, and an end, but the same is not true of a dream. Its dimensions in time and space are quite different; to understand it you must examine it from every aspect—just as you may take an unknown object in your hands and turn it over and over until you are familiar with every detail of its shape.[1]

I always typed a copy of my dreams for Dr. L., so that when we discussed them we could each look at a copy. First, I would tell what had been going on in my outer life at the time, and then I would tell what the dream symbolized to me. Talking it over, Dr. L. would then point out things I had not noticed or understood, and when I felt a click inside, I would know that the interpretation was correct.

It never ceased to amaze me that my outer activities always seemed to lead me into tense personal situations, like falling in love, or its opposite. These interpersonal dynamics were necessary at the time for my inner development. If a situation became a problem, I had to solve it at a new level of awareness without my doctor telling me what to do. It was almost as if the situation itself pressed a button that opened a secret door within me. Out of this inner hidden door would come the symbols in the form of a dream. My analyst and I would discuss these symbols from many different angles, from both a universal and a personal point of view. If it were not yet time for me to understand what was shown to me in the dream, the symbol would return to the place from which it came, and the door would close, maybe to open later, showing the same symbol in a different garb, until I understood what it was telling me.

I did not always take in what my analyst said about my dreams, however, even after I had been in analysis several years. I realize now that I heard only what I was capable of hearing at the time, and that the rest was stored in my unconscious to arise when I had real need of it.

Alan McGlashan says:

> There is in all men, irrespective of age, race, or intellectual power, a function, curiously neglected except for immediate and therapeutic purpose, which is largely independent of human limitations of time and space, and of human structural necessities of thought. I refer to the *Dreaming Mind.* Within this peculiar function, I suggest, there may be concealed the means by which once more the whole world of human consciousness can be levered into a new position. It is at least worth investigation. For without some such asssistance from "outside," contemporary consciousness is plainly on its way towards an unmanageable explosion of ideas, and a fatal loss of the sense of direction.[2]

Thinking about the initial dream I took to my analyst, I can see now that it was a prognosis, a sort of X-ray of my soul. It showed my doctor the possibilities in my psyche in relation to my analysis and individuation.

I was in a Russian custom house, an immigration center, where I had to wait for permission before I could pass into the next country. I was in a large room where someone important was expected. I noticed on a desk some parchment envelopes. I took one and opened it. Inside I found tiny objects of all colors, such as one finds in a Christmas stocking. I took out a tiny figure, a sort of Christ Child, and it was adorable. Then I was summoned to another room to a bureau, and a man gave me a pass with the letters M.O. on it. I said, "My name has four letters, M.V.C.O., not two letters." He said, "You are a couple." I did not answer but signed with the four letters, or initials. I was then in another part of the building with a man friend. A workman was doing something when suddenly a pillar fell in our direction. I felt it was dangerous so we walked out into the street. Then I found myself alone, walking down a heavily wooded mountain trail. In front of me was a woman friend carrying a baby. As the trail switched back and forth, the friend suggested that we sit and slide down, since that would be quicker and we could meet the trail below. I did not agree, as I felt it would be dangerous for the baby.

The immigration center, I learned from my analyst, is a place that marks a transition from a known to an unknown place, probably between the conscious and unconscious worlds. The envelope is a hidden container of personal things or messages. I opened it—the desire to experience the unknown. I found objects of all colors, values, and variations of symbols in my cultural tradition related to Christmas as a form of rebirth. From these I chose the Christ Child, a representation of the innermost seed of my soul, similar to the child of Jung's Stone. Thus, I received permission to pass into the unconscious, but with my conscious cultural identity intact.

I insisted on my four intitials, not two. In this symbolism of the four I showed an unconscious desire to experience not only the conscious and unconscious sides of myself, M.O., but also my cultural heritage and wholeness, the four sides of myself, M.V.C.O., like the four directions of a compass. I had always ignored my middle name, Van Cortlandt, because I felt it was a part of my family's heritage.

The man said: "You are a couple," a precognition of the meaning of the symbolic marriage, "some kind of marriage," as Henry Miller had predicted. Accordingly, I was next with a man friend: my unknown side, the animus. A pillar fell in our direction, and I felt it was dangerous. The pillar, from a non-Freudian point of view, is a support of the world and the house, a universal mother symbol.[3] As I knew I had a mother problem, I felt that somehow the dangerous pillar had to do with her. This pillar had supported my everyday world, the world centered by my ego, and now it was tottering and starting to fall. This falling pillar frightened me, and I walked away, for I was not yet ready to orient my ego to both my worlds, inner as well as outer, outer as well as inner, nor could I face my mother problem. That a male companion was with me hinted that through him my unconscious opposite, my animus, lay the answer to a conscious affinity to my two worlds. The pillar, a threatening symbol in contrast to the Christ Child, represented the archetypal product of a semidivine mother.

Walking down a wooded mountain trail—a spiral path of initiation into the woods—was another aspect of the unconscious. The woman friend, whom I identified, was a more intuitive person and more conscious than I was, because she had already been in analysis a long while. She was a reassuring figure. She was carrying my baby—my new life—as I was not yet ready to carry it myself. She suggested a short cut, but I said no, for it would not be good for the baby. This told my analyst that my intuitive, goal-seeking side might want to take short cuts, but that I wanted to experience this path fully, without cheating or relying on someone else's guidance.

Shortly after I commenced my analysis, I experienced a strong need to be contained, to be protected. So I drew and painted a vase and gave the picture to my doctor, not realizing what it told him. Then in a dream, I slipped into a vase which contained me. This gave me the same feeling I have now when I go into my own house and close the door. I am protected, I am safe.

In the following dream, I was out of the vase and holding it in my hands. It had an octagonal mouth.

I was in an ancient oriental temple going through an initiation. I had to circle the temple and take from each shrine offerings of

leaves, which were of all colors, and put them in the vase in my
hand. I felt that a priest was watching me.

With Dr. L., my medicine man, I moved spirally into the dark,
mysterious, magic world of the unconscious. The "Way" led up
and down and in and out of the stratifications of my unconscious. It was similar to going back through history and re-exper-
iencing the course of evolution. It was difficult, and many times I
felt like giving it all up. I felt like the Sumerian Goddess Inanna,
who had to pass through the seven gates of the Underworld. At
each portal she had to shed one of her worldly garments before
she was allowed to pass on. Finally, she stood naked before the
dreaded Queen of the Underworld. Her sentence was death—
death with no guarantee of rebirth. In the process of individuation, one has to throw away one's personal worldly coverings, as
though they were the tatters of an old personality to be ex-
changed for a new.

During this time, my thoughts often returned to the Stone
and the large circle carved on its face. The circle resembled a
cell, I thought, or an egg, and it seemed to hold everything within
it. The egg is a well known symbol of generation and of the mystery of life. According to various legends, many of the ancient
gods were egg-born: Phanes, the Greek Sun God, who burst out of
the Orphic egg; Eros, who broke through the shell of the egg of
night as it lay floating on the waters of chaos. There were also Re
of the Egyptians, Brahma of the Hindus, First Man in China, and
many others. All of them were egg-born; Mercury, too, was found
in the Philosopher's egg.

The child of the Stone was like a seed, I thought, the germ of
an egg, within the womb-like circle that is a shell. The child may
secretly and inwardly develop within the protective circle and
emerge self-created.

I felt that the mandala face of the Stone gazed at me with a
timeless, hypnotic, searching look. It seemed to be alive. It had a
force all its own which drew me to it like a magnet and yet, in
another way, threw me off like a spinning ball. The ball flattened
and became a wheel that turned. If it were a Tibetan prayer
wheel, I could turn the wheel as I prayed for an answer to the
Stone's significance. The wheel became a cart wheel, and reminded me of an early dream—my first mandala dream.

I saw a huge cart wheel which stood upright and could turn. It had eight spokes and from the outside rim next to each spoke hung eight tools such as a hammer, saw, hatchet, chisel, and screwdriver.

This dream told me that these work tools on the outside rim of the wheel were in my everyday world. In my analysis, I must find the tools in my inner world and learn how to use them consciously. I realized that there was no figure in the center of my own mandala wheel; I knew that the most important part, my treasure, must lie deeply hidden in the depth of the unconscious. Lao Tzu said: "We put thirty spokes together and call it a wheel; but it is on the space where there is nothing that the utility of the wheel depends."[4]

A few months after I had begun my analysis, I was feeling upset and tense, so I decided to try to find out why. I took paper and a pencil and, without thought, I allowed my hand to write. This is what came out, a free association:

Earth—earth—Mother Earth—Birth—birth—birth of what? What will come under the sun? Sunlight—rainbow—sew— sew—sew the rainbow. Bow down—bow up—sup—sup— the last supper—the last together—feather bed—feather mate —fate—fate—hate—hate. What do I hate? Who can it be—bee —see—see—the bumble bee. Bee bite—bee sting—sling shot on the wing. Wings go down—wings go up—who the hell has the guts? Guts for what? Guts where? All wrapped up in woman's hair. Hair down—tied to the ground—cut it off—burn it all—shawl—shawl—my mother's shawl. Wrap her up—roll her tight—bonds to hold her mighty tight. Tight—light—what a sight—groans and wails—body flails—now to weigh it on the scales. Scales of fish—scales of snake—bake—bake—bake the cake. Cake to the sun—the only one—he is high—high in the sky—what a guy.

After I had written the free association, I felt relaxed and peaceful, so I decided to walk with my dog straight up into the hills in back of my house.

The air was fresh from recent showers and beauty was everywhere. The way the Navaho describe it: "Beauty above me, beauty beneath me, beauty all about me, I walk in beauty."

In the spirit of growing things we walked. I was not alone— my shadow was with me. I took a good look at it as it lay on the earth and within me. Climbing, up we went. It was upon Mother

Earth that we walked. Up, over the huge pendulous earth bosoms we stepped, and from above I gazed down onto a full, rounded slope shaped like a vast belly. Mother Nature's womb had given birth to all. Her belly was full and sensuous; from below it the earth-thighs stretched toward the sea. Two full, rounded ridges they were, spread slightly to show her secret place—a ravine, covered with a growth of young pine trees. The thighs lay in full sunlight, but the ravine was shaded. I looked for a "birth" to take place. Maybe a deer would spring from the inner cave hidden by the young trees. The whole earth-body seemed to be writhing in travail.

On returning to the house I immediately wrote down my experience in my dream book. I could hardly wait to take both the free association and my fantasy to my doctor, for I felt something had been born in me. The deer, I knew, was often a symbol of the soul.

Wondering, I asked myself: To what in nature might I compare my analysis?

"Look out your window and what do you see?" a voice asked.

"I see a fruit tree, a nectarine tree, and all I know of this tree is what is visible to me. Before my analysis, I could have said the same about myself."

"Imagine that you are the tree and that, with your analyst's help, you are investigating this tree which is Maud Oakes," the voice said. "This would be comparable in a most general way to your experiencing analysis and individuation. In order to understand the wholeness of the tree, which is yourself and its environment, and to ensure its possibilities, you first have to know what family of tree you came from, the peculiarities of your seed, what it could become, and its patterns of growth."

"Yes!" I thought, "Dr. L. and I are digging down, down beneath the earth, examining my root system to be sure that my roots are not cut off or obstructed."

"Eventually you and your analyst will remove all the main obstructions," the voice continued, "so that the necessary nourishment will flow freely and enable the tree, which is yourself, to grow both beneath and above the earth and to bear its fullness of leaves, flowers, fruits, and seeds."

Thinking about my analysis, I now see clearly its pattern of two distinct divisions. The first part lasted two years. During that time I saw my analyst only one or two times a month, due to my living at a considerable distance from him. By the second year of analysis I had finished the second draft of my book and visited Jung at Bollingen, and it was on my return to Big Sur that I received his last letter containing the criticism that I had asked for. After reading that letter many times, I felt that what Jung was telling me was that my approach to the Stone was too intellectual and lacked feeling. This criticism was valid, and yet I knew that there was more to his censure than what lay on the surface of the letter. It was obvious that I had identified with the Stone and with Jung, and that this identification was interfering with my analysis, but I did not know what to do about it.

I gazed on the Stone in a sort of a trance. I asked myself out loud what to do about the Stone, the book, and my analysis. Again I heard the voice: "I am the Spirit of the Stone. I am as important to you as I was to my carver-creator Jung. Now is the time to turn away from me and rediscover me again within yourself."

"But I need you," I said aloud. "I can't give you up when I have just found you."

"I shall always be here; for I am within you and outside you and all about you, as you will soon know."

So it was that I relinquished my book and its subject matter, the Stone, and put them away for five years, and with confidence gave myself over completely to my analysis. This giving over of myself reminds me again of my experience under LSD. I did not have a deep inner experience at an archetypal level until I had courage enough to overcome my fear of closing my eyes and severing my connections with my everyday world of the senses—a world of intensified colors and movement as experienced under LSD. Closing my eyes was for me an act of sacrifice—the giving up of my ego for an unknown state.

Similarly, it took courage to withdraw my projection from the Stone, to give up the book I had worked on for so long, and to put myself completely in the hands of my doctor. I felt that I was offering up to him not only my ego, but also my most precious possession, my soul. However, that act put me back on the path from which I had strayed. Only when I put aside the book did I have the necessary transference to Dr. L., who had replaced Jung and his Stone in my life. The analyst was not only my human guide, but also my animus in the role of medicine man, priest, and phantom lover. To me he was "my man," the recipient of my deepest feelings. My whole life revolved around him. Jung says:

> The transference phenomenon is an inevitable feature of every thorough analysis, for it is imperative that the doctor should get into the closest possible touch with the patient's line of psychological development . . . [I]n the same measure as the doctor assimilates the intimate psychic contents of the patient into himself, he is in turn assimilated as a figure into the patient's psyche. I say "as a figure," because I mean that the patient sees him not as he really is, but as one of those persons who figured so significantly in his previous history. . . . The transference therefore consists in a number of projections which act as a substitute for a real psychological relationship. They create an apparent relationship and this is very important, since it comes at a time when the patient's habitual failure to adapt has been artificially intensified by his analytical removal into the past.[5]

The most helpful and creative aspect of my analysis was this transference made to my doctor and his counter-transference to me. I felt an unconscious flow between us and instinctively knew that we were experiencing together what I was going through. The relationship expressed itself in a dream:

> *I was in a hotel with Dr. L. He led me out of the lobby with people into an inner room where we made love on a couch. I noticed that nearby was another couple making love.*

This part of the dream showed me that I had made a transference to my doctor. The other couple making love emphasized the universal nature of the transference, to correct the idea that it was uniquely personal. Next:

> *I was walking along a path with an elderly woman. She led me into a hogan. Inside was sitting an elderly Navaho medicine man. He said: "You are a virgin and I shall break your hymen for you." Then he held me under a blanket and explored my vagina. I wondered if the woman had led me to him for this.*

"For the feminine, the act of defloration represents a truly mysterious bond between end and beginning, between ceasing to be and entering upon real life."[6]

Then I was in Siberia with some couples bundling. I was between two men. The man on my right made love to me. Then I met a man friend and he said: "Maud, take this." He took a match stick with cotton on the end of it. He dipped it in the saliva in his mouth and then into my mouth.

This showed transformation from a biological level to a spiritual.

An Indian Rajah lived near me in an apartment. He saw people only by appointment. When he was out, I went to his apartment and pretended I was the maid and let appointees in. Then he returned and caught me as myself. I found him young and very attractive. When he kissed me on the mouth he seemed to engulf me. We both enjoyed it.

The Rajah here symbolized the power of consciousness. At this time I had much more confidence in myself and awareness in relation to what my dreams were telling me. Yet I knew I had a long way to go.

Then I had a dream that I shared a house with my doctor and it was natural. Then an older man, whom I did not know, said he was marrying me.

It took a long time for me to understand the significance of these special dreams. When I commenced to see clearly what they were telling me, the transference began to dissolve, very slowly. My analyst was wise enough to allow this to happen by helping me to understand my dreams, which told him what was going on. Just the same, I still needed the transference in order to get rid of my negative mother complex—as was shown in the following dream:

I was told that an initiator would come. I lay on a camp cot high in the hills. He came and things happened. We made love. Then I was in a dark room with the initiator. A white object like a stone, connected with initiation, fell from above to the floor and as it fell I saw attached to it by a thread a black widow spider. The initiator turned into a man friend and together we killed the spider.

The spider, I was told, represented the negative mother complex.

Later on a voice in a dream told me that Dr. L. had died. Death is one of the symbols of resolution of transference dependency. Even though I knew it signified that my transference had ended, the news was exceedingly upsetting to me. I did not tell Dr. L. of the dream until a year later, as I feared I might lose him. Although my inner dependency on my doctor had ended and we had become good friends, I still had need of him to help me understand an important dream that would remain with me until I fully comprehended its message. Then would come a wonderful feeling of clarity, almost as if I saw the dream under intense light.

Jung says:

> The transference phenomenon is without doubt one of the most important syndromes in the process of individuation; its wealth of meanings goes far beyond mere personal likes and dislikes. By virtue of its collective contents and symbols it transcends the individual personality and extends into the social sphere, reminding us of those higher human relationships which are so painfully absent in our present social order, or rather disorder.[7]

An important phase of my inward journey was now behind me. But my guide, too, was behind me. I seemed for a time to be alone—quite alone—but not for long.

CHAPTER

VII

The Inner Way

A Zen Master describes the Way:

The great path has no gates,
Thousands of roads enter it.
When one passes through this gateless gate
He walks freely between heaven and earth.[1]

All life is a series of stages of individual growth which encompasses man's body and soul. He can experience the series fully, or be stopped in his development anywhere along the way. Jung's individuation process is usually experienced after middle age or toward the end of life. It is not a withdrawal from life, but life itself—a way between man-the-seen and his soul-the-unseen. It is a way of death-and-rebirth, transformation toward experiencing wholeness. In analysis, the analytical psychologist knows whether the patient is ready for the individuation process and whether he or she is equal to it; for like the initiations of old, the way is dangerous and difficult, and not all analysands need or want such a drastic change to take place.

Jung said about individuation: "The meaning and the purpose of the process is the realization, in all its aspects, of the personality originally hidden away in the embryonic germ-plasm; the production and unfolding of the original, potential wholeness."[2]

To find this wholeness, my challenge was to bring together into a relationship the two sides of my nature—inner and outer, spiritual and material. Throughout the long period of time that I had worked with my analyst, I had talked only to a few close friends about this secret inner experience—only to those whom I knew would understand. To me, individuation was an initiation, a sacred experience that should not be discussed. Also, I did not want to open myself to the criticism of family and friends who might label me mentally sick or apart from life. How strange that it is taken for granted that man can travel to the moon and can delve into other worlds on drugs, yet some people still consider it abnormal for anyone to enter analysis in order to explore regions of the psyche.

I have always felt that life is an endless series of tests and trials to be confronted and surmounted as we go on our "way." When I finally recognized that my Peruvian accident was such a test and tried to understand its meaning, the way to the Stone opened for me. That I recognized it as an Opener of the Door, and consciously did something about it, led me on my "way," a psychological way of a profoundly transforming nature. I knew there were other processes, for I had tried some. I was also aware of the natural way, an unconscious way, similar to nature herself who develops without thought.

Looking back to an inner experience I had back in New Mexico in the early 1940s while working with Navaho medicine men, I now see that that experience was a preliminary step toward individuation. At the time, I was recording sand paintings and myths given to me by old Wilito, a well-known medicine man. One morning he suggested that he perform a Purifying Rite over me. "It is the same Blessing Way ceremony that the gods gave over 'Changing Woman,'" he said. "It will drive the white man's poison out of you and then I can give you prayers and paintings without danger to you or to me." I was delighted with his suggestion and accepted the unknown event with excitement.

The whole deeply moving experience lasted two nights and one day. I felt completely out of time and not myself. The first night and continuing on throughout the ceremony, myths having to do with the earth goddess, Changing Woman, were expressed in song form, and prayers were said over me. I was continually blessed. My body was pressed by Wilito with the Talking Prayer Sticks and the heavy bag containing the sands of the four Holy Mountains. The goal was to drive the white man's poison out of me. I ate enough holy pollen to line my intestinal tract.

The next day, after Wilito and the others had had sweat baths, I was told to wait outside the hogan. At a signal, I entered and saw that a white corn pollen path had been made from the doorway to where the medicine man sat and on around to the right, ending with the symbol of female lightning. From this same path another branched off in the center of the hogan and led to a round sand platform, a symbol of the universe, on which stood the ceremonial basket.

On the path that lay before me, four yellow cornmeal foot-steps had been made. I stepped on them with great care and arrived at the basket, where I knelt on two pollen crosses that symbolized strength to my mind, so that I would always think positively in the four directions. There a lovely Navaho woman gave me a ceremonial bath from my head to the soles of my feet. In the basket, suds had been made with four yucca stems and leaves and herbs. Wilito dried me with yellow cornmeal.

I put on the clean clothes I had brought with me. Wilito sprinkled special holy pollen in my moccasins so that I would walk straight on my Life Path. All night long, Wilito sang out his power, with the other men joining in until sleep overcame them. I seemed to be transported to another world.

At the approach of dawn, Wilito instructed me what to do as he handed me his holy pollen bag. I went outside into the cool dark dawn with just a streak of light showing to the east. With the pollen bag in my right hand, I said my prayer to the God of the Dawn. With arms outspread I brought the bag to my face four times, breathing in its strength and purity. And four times I sprinkled pollen on my head, on my tongue, and out into nature and to the God of Dawn and the Gods of the Navaho universe.

When I reentered the hogan, Wilito gave me a new name, "Gleniba," she who walks with her friends. I felt free, washed clean of my negative, material world, and very insignificant, yet one with Changing Woman, with nature, and with the Navaho himself. I was on my "Way."

The word "way" is reminiscent of the Chinese concept of the Tao, which means the "Way," the "Inner Way," the "Meaning of the World." Jung found a great similarity between the Taoists' definition of the psyche and his own. He said of their philosophy:

> It is built on the premise that the cosmos and man, in the last analysis, obey the same law; that man is a microcosm and is not separated from the macrocosm by any fixed barriers. The very same laws rule for the one as for the other, and from the

one a way leads into the other. The psyche and the cosmos are to each other like the inner world and the outer world. Therefore man participates by nature in all cosmic events, and is inwardly as well as outwardly interwoven with them.[3]

That is what I experienced on LSD the second and last time I took it. I saw only a great weaving of horizontal and vertical lines in vivid colors that moved up and down and in and out. And I felt no fear, for I somehow knew I was a part of the great woven tapestry of life—part of the whole.

Jung discovered that in following the way of individuation, man meets and experiences certain archetypes. Some of the most common of these are the Shadow, the Animus or Anima, the Wise Old Man, the Great Mother, and the Self. These archetypes belong to the historical soul of man. Those that I encountered were Openers of the Door for me. I contacted them neither through my senses nor as actual entities, but rather as symbolic projections from the depth of my soul. To me a symbol can have various meanings, quite in contrast to a conventional man-made *sign* that represents only an idea. The archetypal symbols act as transporters of energy from the unconscious into the conscious mind. Nor is that the end of it. I soon discovered that each archetype I encountered was many-faceted, and its symbolic projections could appear again and again in different guises, according to my development and need throughout the course of my life.

In trying to describe what the archetypes symbolized for me, I shall present them in the order in which Jungians usually present them. However, I actually encountered no special order of progression, with the exception of the Shadow, which came first (probably because it lived in my personal unconscious), and the Self, which came at the end that is not the end. The rest of the archetypes lay mixed together in the depth of my psyche. They were the transformers of energy from my unconscious into my conscious mind. According to my need, the projected symbols appeared again and again in dreams or fantasies, or on objects in my everyday life, until I saw through their countless guises.

Although I had recorded my dreams for almost thirty years and painted those that seemed most important to me at the time, it was not until I was well along in my analysis that I saw a dream pattern of development. As I progressed in my inner and outer involvement, I commenced interpreting my dreams by myself, encouraged by my analyst. If I came to a block, I would consult him about it. At times my recollection of his dream interpretations seemed to vanish after I left his office.

Now I realize I was not yet receptive to what the dream symbols were telling me. Yet, without my being aware of it, the symbols had taken hold of me and remained in my unconscious mind for days and weeks until, like a flash of lightning, I understood what they were telling me. In this way the contents of my unconscious merged with my conscious mind, and out of this oneness came a transformation. Jung's term for this transformation is *the transcendent function.*

I discovered that the symbols of individuation are similar to what man has always experienced in his initiations into the ancient mysteries, so I felt like a neophyte undergoing a rite of passage, an aspirant for initiation into the mysteries of the individuation process. This "inner way" was a solitary way, unprotected and uncontained, except for my relationships with Dr. L. and a few friends.

Henderson wrote that initiation for a man is different than for a woman. He is the hero who has to kill the dragon of the underworld, an ordeal and trial of strength. For a woman it is the gradual realization of her identity as a woman, an awakening to consciousness.

> On the other hand, the woman, no less than the man, has her initial trials of strength [similar to the hero journey] that lead to a final sacrifice for the sake of experiencing the new birth. This sacrifice enables a woman to free herself from the entanglement of personal relations and fits her for a more conscious role as an individual in her own right. In contrast, a man's sacrifice is a surrender of his sacred independence: He becomes more consciously related to woman.[4]

It is not easy for me to describe the opening stage of my initiation, since in the beginning I was so unconscious—unaware of what was taking place within me. All I know is that when I left New York and my life there for New Mexico and the Navaho Indians, I had already entered on my Path, and I am now convinced that it all came about because I accepted the Opener of the Door that was offered me, apparently by chance.

It happened at a dinner I attended in early 1941 in honor of Frau Froebe-Kapteyn, a Dutch woman, who founded the Eranos conferences held yearly in Switzerland. During the dinner Frau Froebe remarked that she was astonished that so few Americans were aware of their great heritage in the American Indians and their fascinating myths.

Without thought I spoke up. "I am very much aware of the mythology of the Indians," I said, "and I would give anything to be able to record the myths and sand-paintings of the Navaho."

After dinner the head of the Old Dominion Foundation asked me if I really wanted to work with the Navaho, for if I did I could apply for a grant. When I asked eagerly for more details, he said, "All you have to do is to write a letter to the Foundation, explaining what you want to do and giving your qualifications."

"I have none," I said.

"Just write down what you think your assets are," he said.

So, after much deliberation, I wrote the letter, with no expectations, and listed what I considered to be my assets. I was an artist, I wrote, a painter; hence my facilities for observation were good. I had no feeling of prejudice nor fear of being alone, which was important. It was an asset that I was untrained as an ethnologist, as I was free to allow things to happen and, besides, I was a good automobile mechanic.

Within a week I received a letter of acceptance from the Foundation. I was amazed at my good fortune. Many years later I learned that the directors had been amused by my list of qualifications and had decided to give me a chance. Little did I know that I was not only accepting a grant, but also a definite challenge out of which would come a new life. Nor did I foresee that the fruits of the Navaho adventure of three years would eventually be two books, an exhibition of my personal paintings of Navaho myths and drawings of medicine men at the Willard Gallery in New York, and another exhibition of Navaho sand and pollen paintings at the National Gallery of Art in Washington, D.C.

In 1941 I lived for six months on the outskirts of the Navaho reservation, twenty-two miles from Gallup, New Mexico, before the Indians accepted me. This finally came about after they saw my paintings illustrating some of their fascinating myths; I hung them on my hogan wall. They were executed in earth colors, in a way the Navaho understood. Also, every night I prayed for aid. Speaking out loud, I said, "Please, God, make me open to receive and to be egoless." What I was doing without being aware of it was having a dialogue with my unconscious, so that I, my ego, could utilize its energy and wisdom. Out of this new approach came an answer—the dream I told Jung when I visited him at Küsnacht in 1953.

In the dream I was sitting nude on yellow female pollen in a holy medicine basket. The Navaho Wind God was looking down at me. When I told this dream to the medicine man I was working with at the time, he said, "It is a good dream. If you were a Navaho I would give a prayer over you." "What difference does it make, I would like a prayer," I said. So he recited the prayer sprinkling me with holy pollen as he gave it. It was then and during the Purifying Rite that my femininity was born and I removed my mask, or the persona, as Jung calls it, and became myself. The Indians felt this and accepted me as a friend, a woman friend they could trust.

This first mask that I took off was what I felt the world wanted me to be. When it was on, I acted the part the mask depicted, but when I took it off it was like removing my clothes; I was myself. I now see that my mask had developed as my ego had grown. It was a facade that I gradually added to myself, like a facade on a house. I know that such a mask is often necessary in the material world I live in, serving as a buffer between me and society.

I well remember removing my mask when I entered Dr. L.'s office for the first time. I was uneasy and felt like a snail without its shell. So, like a defenseless snail, I began my analysis. At first I felt as if I were floating on a sea of unconsciousness, afraid to relinquish the objects of my outer world to which I was clinging. I had to remove my mask knowingly and let go and be aware of what I was doing in order to pass the threshold into the underworld of my unconscious. Only after what seemed like eons of time did I gradually began to know when I was in masquerade— and also what other people were hiding behind. Then I was ready to enter the stratum of my personal unconscious, and engage in the encounter with the Shadow.

Eliot wrote:

> *For Thine is the Kingdom*

> Between the conception
> And the creation
> Between the emotion
> And the response
> Falls the shadow

> *Life is very long*

> Between the desire
> And the spasm
> Between the potency
> And the existence
> Between the essence
> And the descent
> Falls the shadow. . . .[5]

Symbolically, the personal unconscious was a dark and difficult land ruled over by the shadow and the waning moon, like the moon on Jung's Stone, since, being a woman, my shadow is female. When I was well along in my analysis, I began to see the projections of my shadow in dreams, in my everyday life, even in words that seemed to come right out of me unbidden. One after another, these shadow symbols were all aspects of the hidden life that I had buried in my unconscious. Often I projected them onto mother figures or female friends, since it was more than a challenge to my ego to have to see and admit to myself that precisely what I criticized and could not bear in friends was usually the shadow-side of myself.

I was critical not only of friends but also of some Jungian-oriented women who had finished their analyses. "What has it done for them?" I would ask myself, or I would say, "I see little improvement." I was observing not only their shadows, but also the projection of my own dark side onto them. At such times I would become very negative and decide to stop my analysis, as I felt it was a waste of time. What I should have realized was that we are all different, and that the possibility for development depends on where we are and what we are doing about it.

The first shadow dream that I understood was about a woman I hardly knew. I saw her as aggressive. She radiated power, and I disliked her.

I saw her coming along a city street towards me. I quickly hid
and she passed by without seeing me.

My analyst asked me what I thought of her. "She is a bulldozer," I
said. Suddenly I realized that I myself was often this type of bulldozer, and it shocked me. No wonder I disliked her. Another type
of woman that I could not bear was the very feminine and insin-
cere type who disliked and undermined every female in her orbit.

Five years later, I had a dream that showed me what my
challenge was. My dark side had to be awakened with feeling; I
had to give life to my unconscious and bring out my dark side,
the shadow.

In my dream I saw a figure lying on a divan against the wall. It
was covered by a very dark blanket. I pulled the blanket off and
lay on top of the figure, my shadow pressing my face with feeling
against the other face.

A month later, I had a very important dream that indicated that
the shadow could be redeemed.

I was on a boat at sea. Everyone knew there was a woman spy on
board and she must be liquidated. They offered her poison in a
glass, but she would not take it. They asked me to offer it to her.
I did and she drank it. She asked me if she had taken poison, and
I said, "Yes." "Thank God," she said with feeling, and we em-
braced. Then I saw a woman who lay on the earth about to die. I
told people I would bring her back to life. A friend came along, a
shadow figure for me. She was a doctor and I became her assis-
tant. In a tube of clear water I put drops of black water. Then I
was walking along a city street, a man came towards me and
said, "One has to die to be reborn," and I said, "Yes."

The shadow often arouses suspicion that can only be allayed
by an awakening of love. Putting the drops of black water into
clear water showed me that I was aware of the dark, evil side of
my shadow. This leads to death and rebirth, an archetype to be
activated as a precondition not only of redemption of the shadow, but also of atonement.

An integral part of individuation is the theme of death for rebirth. It entails great suffering and a strong desire to attain a new
approach to life, a new personality, and, finally, inner and outer
freedom. During this period I had many different death dreams. I
also had a feeling that I was being crucified, and naturally related

it to Dr. L. Was my analysis at this point becoming too sacrificial, martyring me?

I subsequently went through a very negative period in which I felt I was all alone on an empty desert. I decided to stop my analysis, feeling that it was a waste of time and money. I had accepted an invitation from the C. G. Jung Institute in Zurich to give a seminar. There I met Dora Kalff, a well-known Swiss therapist who has done extraordinary work with children. Sensing that she was an Opener of the Door, I decided to work with her. Before taking this step, I consulted Dr. L., who was in Zurich at the time. He thought it was an excellent idea, knowing it would be therapeutic for me to work with a woman as a positive mother figure.

Dora Kalff usually uses a sandbox for her treatments. This held no appeal for me, so she gave me water color crayons and large pieces of wrapping paper and seated me at a good-sized table. She sat in the corner of the room like a Buddha, and never said a word to me. She was like a medicine woman or shaman. Now and then I was oblivious of her; at other times I was aware of her healing presence. I worked with her one hour a day for five days, and the results were quite amazing.

On my return from Europe, I sensed a new awareness within me and a feeling of solidity and centeredness. Also, I became more conscious of my projections of my mother onto women friends. This resolved my inner fear of women, and I was able to relate to them more easily. My cousin Jerome told me that he saw a great change in me. With this encouragement, I resumed my work with Dr. L. Going over some previous shadow dreams with him, I realized and accepted the fact that what I call my shadow will always be with me, but learning to see its projections clearly can diminish and somewhat control its power over me.

Translating Lao Tzu, Arthur Waley writes:

Endless the series of things without name
On the way back to where there is nothing.
They are called shapeless shapes;
Forms without form;
Are called vague semblances.
Go towards them, and you can see no front;
Go after them, and you see no rear.

Yet by seizing on the Way that was
You can ride the things that are now.
For to know what once there was, in the Beginning,
This is called the essence of the Way.[6]

My next test was to face and recognize the unconscious masculine side of myself, my unknown man-enemy-friend, the negative animus. According to Jung, the feminine aspect of a man, the anima, produces *moods*, while the male aspects of a woman, the animus, produces *opinions*. ". . . [As] the moods of a man issue from a shadowy background, so the opinions of a woman rest on equally unconscious prior assumptions."[7]

It took many years of work with my analyst before I began to recognize the different disguises of my animus, both negative and positive, evil and good, and to accept what I saw. I had not only to recognize my animus, but to see and comprehend how it acted out in my daily life. I had to be careful not to identify with these projections and also to be constantly aware of what they symbolized and of how they affected me. Otherwise, my animus could possess me and turn me into a bossy, masculine type of "you-can't-tell-me-anything" woman, instead of relating itself to me as to a feminine human being. I also had to be constantly aware that the animus is an unconscious autonomous power that roams at will throughout my psyche, and that it is only animus projections that can be experienced and consciously integrated.

I remember a dream I had when I was living with the Mam Indians of Guatemala. I had been with them six months, and was trying to establish a rapport with them and particularly with the shamans, the medicine men. Every night I prayed for help, and finally it came.

It was night and I was in a sort of village square. On my right was a fountain with no water in it. A very old man approached me, dressed in the Mam costume, and he said: "I want you to take the male lead in a play that I am going to present." I said, "But how can I take the male lead when I am a woman?" He repeated what he had said. I looked down and saw I was dressed in a Mam Indian male costume, so I agreed. At that moment water began to rise upward in the fountain (source of the waters of life).

The old man must have been the Wise Old Man who is an aspect of the animus. He was telling me that by recognizing the helpful animus within me, I would be able to contact the Indians and their medicine men and shamans. This is just what happened, for the Indians finally sensed something different in me and accepted me as a friend. Furthermore, I became the doctor of the village and so, in their eyes, became a medicine man.

Another very important animus dream was the following:

> I was trying to unscrew the top of a cistern that was buried in the earth. Only the lid showed and it was round with a square nut in the center. I used a wrench, turning to the left. An old man, a plumber, came along and asked if he could help me. I thanked him, saying I had already opened it. When I looked inside I saw many flower bulbs of all colors and sizes. They were Oriental and ready for planting. I took the largest, which fascinated me. It already had two roots opposite one another. I asked the plumber, who had turned into a gardner, how to plant it. He said, "The two things are not roots but necessary, for when planted, roots would grow between them."

Since I am at heart a gardener, I felt this was an excellent dream. In fact, the dream is always with me, and at times it becomes a reality. Bulbs belong to the World Mother, Earth, and are full of the mysterious potentialities of life. I am always amazed at the many layers of skin that make up their texture, and I am very much aware of their downward and upward growth, producing first roots and then stem, leaves, buds, and flowers, like bringing together the opposites to form a oneness—what an amazing Self-symbol, which is not only the seed of the psyche but also its wholeness.

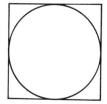 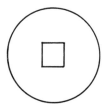

On Jung's Stone the circle is in the square, signifying that through the "squaring of the circle" wholeness, or oneness, has been achieved. In my dream, the square nut was in the center of the circle, the opposite of Jung's Stone. This indicated that I must turn the nut to the left toward the unconscious to find what was buried in the container, in the earth, both of which are mother symbols.

A plumber asked whether he could help, a projection of my unconscious animus, he who works underground controlling the water and the sewers, or my unconscious instinctive energy, both positive and negative. I looked inside the container and found flower bulbs. I chose one that had two roots opposite one another. I asked advice of the plumber, who had turned into a gardener, a much more conscious, creative, spiritual animus, he who tends from above what has been planted in the earth. The two things were not roots, he said, they were opposites, but roots could grow between. So the dream was telling me that in my unconscious lies the Self, symbolized by the bulb, which is a creative aspect of the feminine. If with the aid of my animus I could become aware of this, transformation would take place by the downward and upward growth so that the bulb would flower above the earth into the light of day, bringing the two sides of my nature together into "wholeness."

My father, grandfather, brother, and cousin Jerome were very positive figures for me in my early formative years. Not only did they unconsciously help shape my animus, but also by their influence they enabled me to have good relationships with the men in my life who replaced them. The Navaho and Mam Indian men were also very positive animus figures for me.

In particular, my cousin Jerome was a great help. He had a way of saying to no one in particular, "Maud is in her bug-voice mood." This described the way I spoke with a hard, loud voice whenever I saw a large insect or any unusual phenomenon. It expressed an animus-driven woman. After many years, I finally heard what Jerome had been saying and tried to do something about it. My test was to strive to reach a place where my animus became a function of relationship to the unconscious. It was not easy to accomplish this. It required staying on an even keel and being constantly aware of all my shortcomings. I also had to foster a deep feeling for my other half, my animus, even to the point of visualizing him and talking to him the way I would to an intimate friend or a lover. Then he usually responded by becoming a helpful, creative partner.

My "Way" next led from the stratum of the animus-anima into the depth of the collective unconscious. The path spiraled downward into the awesome abyss, the deep, black fathomless world of the archetypes, perhaps a world beyond the fourth dimension. The collective unconscious is the storehouse shared by all mankind. It contains the archetypes formed by man's evolutionary growth of body-mind and spirit-soul.

Due to some integration of my animus, I had to be acutely aware of the danger of inflation—inflation of my ego. It could become possessed by the archetype of God-likeness, which Jung calls the mana personality. I had to watch for the emergence of any feelings of superiority or special wisdom, as I could be dominated by the idea that I was a great spiritual teacher, one who held all the answers, or I might even feel that I embodied the essence of saintliness. If this happened, I would lose all that I had gained in my experiences with the other half of my animus.

I have known both men and women who feel they are great teachers, the unique dispensers of knowledge, or in a minor role they worship at the feet of their so-called masters; but I was hypnotized by the mana personality of the Great Mother herself, the image of all mothers and maidens from the first existence of man and woman. The facets of this great matriarchal image and the myths that surround her oscillate between good and evil. She is the powerful, suffocating, wise, magic, devouring, loving, evil, Earth Goddess. Meeting her in dreams and in everyday life filled me with awe and wonder, yet something always warned me to be on my guard. It was not easy for me to recognize her many forms in my dreams and to know when she was or was not my real mother, probably because my personal mother complex had been deeply rooted in the mother archetype.

In the past I had been a sacrifice to the Great Mother. My challenge now was to do some positive things to make up for my initial rejection of the Mother. So it was up to me to be constantly aware of her magic powers and to try to assimilate her lovely human femininity. Openness, vigilance, deep humility, and the feeling of an inner stability were the weapons I learned to use against the devastating power of her elemental force—which could have transformed me into an inflated, arrogant, "know-it-all" woman, like some of those who have wrongly understood the Women's Liberation Movement and have become possessed, therefore, by the animus. When this happens, a woman loses the strongest tool she has, her own feminine judgment.

So I protected my ego from being seized and taken over by the mana personality, and made every effort to see through and comprehend its symbolic projections, aware that, if I succeeded, I would be free of the Mother and would really know myself. I had many dreams about my mother. Two were most important. The first showed the commencement of liberation, and the second connoted complete freedom from my mother.

> *I was in China living with a married Chinese couple and the woman's mother. I went into the mother's bedroom. She showed me a pistol, saying, "It is my time to go so that my daughter can take her rightful place." The husband of the girl took me to see some distant mountains. On my return we found the mother dead, stretched out on a bed-shelf. We all felt happy, as we knew it was right.*

Many years later I had the second dream, a very clear liberation dream that showed the helpful animus:

> *I was standing upright supporting a stretcher on which lay my mother. She was dead, and completely wrapped in white like a mummy. Two men came along and relieved me of the stretcher and my mother.*

After this second dream came a wonderful feeling of wholeness, the mingling of my inner and outer natures.

Jung says:

> Thus the dissolution of the mana-personality through conscious assimilation of its contents leads us, by a natural route, back to ourselves as an actual, living something, poised between two world-pictures and their darkly discerned potencies. This "something" is strange to us and yet so near, wholly ourselves and yet unknowable, a virtual center of so mysterious a constitution that it can claim anything—kinship with beasts and gods, with crystals and with stars—without moving us to wonder, without even exciting our disapprobation. This 'something' claims all that and more, and having nothing in our hands that could fairly be opposed to these claims, it is surely wiser to listen to this voice.
>
> I have called this center the *self*. Intellectually the self is no more than a psychological concept, a construct that serves

to express an unknowable essence which we cannot grasp as
such, since by definition it transcends our powers of comprehension. It might equally well be called the "God within us."
The beginnings of our whole psychic life seem to be inextrica-
bly rooted in this point, and all our highest and ultimate pur-
poses seem to be striving towards it. This paradox is unavoid-
able, as always, when we try to define something that lies
beyond the bourn of our understanding.[8]

Eliot says:

At the still point of the turning world. Neither flesh nor
    fleshless;
Neither from nor towards; at the still point, there the dance is,
But neither arrest nor movement. And do not call it fixity,
Where past and future are gathered. Neither movement from
    nor towards,
Neither ascent nor decline. Except for the point, the still point,
There would be no dance, and there is only the dance.
I can only say, *there* we have been: but I cannot say where.
And I cannot say, how long, for that is to place it in time.[9]

CHAPTER
VIII

A Conversation
with Hermes

After seven years of analysis, five years of which passed without my thinking of the Stone, I finally decided to finish the book. Even though I had put it aside and given myself over to the process of analysis, the Stone still exerted its original fascination. Not only was there a strong inner tie between us, but I knew that the research I had done on the Stone was somehow a part of me and of my analysis, and would help me understand more about my own intricate nature.

I knew that my next step was to re-experience the symbolism of the Stone. Because of my work with Dr. L., I could now comprehend the Stone's cryptic carvings with a new level of awareness that came from the experience of seeing and trying to understand what had evolved from within me. As I looked at the familiar manuscript with the idea of rewriting it, I understood how wise Jung had been to hint at and point out to me my need for analysis. Not only had he seen and understood the importance of the Stone for my own inner development, but he had also seen the necessity of analysis for any interpreter of his Stone's hidden messages and symbols. I remembered a remark Jung had made to me the last time I had seen him at Bollingen: "The Stone does not belong to me. You might have come by boat and stepped into the garden to photograph it." In relation to the Stone, I knew that Jung was telling me that at this deep archetypal level, what had meaning for him also had meaning for me and for all people.

I was not surprised to find that I no longer had need of the photograph of the Stone. The carvings on it that belonged to me were already engraved inside me, although they had still to be understood. With the aid of the child Mercury-Hermes, they would rise to consciousness as I had need of them. By now my relation to the little figure had changed. I knew instinctively that Mercury-Hermes was intimately related to me, so I decided to call him Hermes. He was no longer just Jung's Mercury, but was also my version of Hermes and the most important clue to finding my treasure. He would be the emissary between my two worlds; my challenge was to see and comprehend what he told me.

In seeking to discover what Hermes symbolized, I imagined that he was a many-faceted jewel that lay in the depth of the unconscious of all mankind. Each projection of this Hermes into consciousness and the behavior pattern associated with him was then but a reflection in time and space of one of the countless facets of this archetype.

"What facets of you do I already know?" I asked, as I visualized him standing in the center of Jung's Stone. And I seemed to hear him reply, "By the sign on my body you can see that I am Hermes-Mercury and I am also Telesphorus. I am both beginning and end, and like a seed I can be self-created."

"You are not only my spirit-messenger," I told him, "but the point between the opposites, like a bridge that joins the land on both banks of a river. Also, you are the energy that can itself cross and recross this bridge, synthesizing the opposites. Maybe you are the goal-less goal of individuation, the Self, though I personally do not believe in goals."

And he answered, "Yes, I am all this for some people and much more, which you will gradually discover as you go within yourself. I shall lead the way, and the lantern I carry will bring light to what you will have to face and experience in your unconscious."

"If you are Jung's treasure, the Self," I asked, "what are you to me?"

But before he could answer, I remembered a dream that I had had shortly after starting my analysis:

I was trying to find out about an important older man. I opened a large, thick book to a picture on a page. The picture was of a carving of a white piece of drapery hung between two uprights covering something unknown to me. Under the picture the cap-

tion read: "This man had most to do with removing the white covering. He was the builder of his house; he was the house and he was not the house; he was everything; in fact, he was Mercury."

"Now I know who you are. You are my other half," I said to Hermes. "Yours is the little voice that speaks from within me, the voice I have called on and listened to for so many years. When I realized that you were Jung's symbol for the Self, it did not surprise me, since the whole feeling of the Stone has pointed to this. But I am more than astonished to discover that you, the child Hermes, are my other half, because I unconsciously adopted you the first time I saw you in Jung's garden at Bollingen."

"You are only partly correct," Hermes answered. "At present, I am with you because you have at last untangled me from your shadow. Now I am your little voice that speaks from within, but not the one that spoke to you in the past. Also, I am and I am not the Mercury that you refer to in your dream. As you have discovered, I am the Spirit of the Stone, but whether or not I am the Self for Jung is none of your concern. This mysterious secret was shared only by Jung and myself."

Thinking again about the dream and the message it contained, I found that the dream was suddenly clarified and was without a doubt an early forecast of my analysis. The important man who had had most to do with removing the white drapery was, of course, Jung. He was the builder of his own house. Yes, he had probed and excavated his inner cellar. Rock by rock, he had laid his foundation, and beam by beam, with a center ridge pole, his inner house had risen. Light, sunlight, entered through windows and a skylight. There were two doors front and back, and a stove that heated the house; the upper floor and cellar were joined by a stairway. Probably the carvings on the Stone commemorated this special house. He was the house—Jung, the man—and he was not the house; he was also the Spirit of the Stone, Mercury.

During the time that I worked on my book, the Stone, and my analysis, Jung had been my animus in the role of doctor, wise man, and carrier of my Self. He had the power to remove the white drapery and expose the unknown something, the treasure that lay between the opposites, if I should become conscious enough to recognize what would then be shown to me. When I put the book away for five years and turned away from the Stone and its carver, Dr. L. took over Jung's role until a voice told me in a dream that my analyst had died. When that happened, Hermes became the carrier of the Self.

"Yes!" I said, "I can now see that you took Dr. L.'s place and that you are the Spirit of the Stone. In my research, I have discovered that you are a varied God. In fact, you are all things to all men. As you are the bearer of my projections, a new world will be opened to me which I must explore without analysis, but with you, Hermes, as my guide. You have been my unthanked assistant, and I still depend on you to help me unveil the riddle of the Stone."

"I am the Spirit of that Stone. When Jung carved the Stone," said Hermes, "he drew forth from within himself the symbols that pertained to his own life experience. He told you this himself when he said, 'I need not have written any books; it is all on the Stone.' Well, I am the Spirit of that Stone, but archetypes, as you know, have countless interpretations. They speak to mankind on many different levels."

"You are suggesting to me that there could be more than one answer to the riddle of the Stone, depending on the seeker and where he stands on his life path?"

"That is correct. And since you recognized me as an Opener of the Door when you first saw me at Bollingen, I can now convey to you clues about the meaning of the Stone that apply to you, yourself. I can do this only if you ask for them, and if you not only recognize them when they appear, but also do something consciously about them."

"I have already been doing that for a long time," I said.

"Yes! With your analyst's help and mine," he answered. "Tell me what you think you have discovered about my Stone in your research."

Closing my eyes, I pictured the four—three zig-zag and one serpentine—lines that connect the two circles of the Stone. They radiate and vibrate and are so full of energy that they seem to be alive. Jung had said that three of the lines were reminiscent of lightning, and the undulating one, of a river or a serpent.

To me, lightning is both exciting and frightening, and it proclaims the rains to come. I picture Jupiter, serenely seated on his

celestial throne, throwing his thunderbolts earthward to enlighten or chastise his earthly victims. The Navaho believe that
lightning is the voice of the gods, to be revered and feared. If
lightning strikes near a Navaho, his house, or his stock, a purifying rite is performed to expel the destructive force that has entered his body or his possessions. Symbolically and psychologically, lightning is a flash of illumination or intuition, but it also
represents forces both fecundating and destructive that can leap
unbidden right out of the unconscious.

As to serpents, they terrify, yet they also fascinate and repel.
Rattlesnakes are found at Big Sur. I learned to watch where I
stepped, lest I disturb one and provoke an attack. The Navaho
never kill a snake, since they believe that a god might inhabit its
body. That serpents move without legs in an undulating manner,
that they are cold-blooded, and can strike, bite, and kill, make
them a perfect symbol for the dark unconscious life of man. As
a symbol of psychic energy, the serpent can both destroy and
transform and, therefore, is a common symbol of transcendence.
Often the serpent is a mother symbol.

In Kundalini Yoga, a female serpent is pictured asleep, coiled
at the base of the human spine near the sexual center, or *chakra*.
In Yoga, it is awakened and symbolically ascends the spine to the
top of the head, passing through six *chakras* until it unites in
the highest and last center, the seventh, with the Lord Siva. This
Kundalini energy is of a spiritual, transforming nature, an up-
lifting of consciousness and the transmutation of creative energy
from the depths to the heights of heaven. And so the practice of
Kundalini Yoga can be compared to the process of individuation,
as it emerges from the depths of unconsciousness.

I regard the serpent as both negative and positive. It had
played a very important role in my analysis. It appeared many

times in dreams until I was aware of what it was telling me, and only then did it leave me alone. About a month after I had begun my analysis, I had the following dream:

> *I was walking along a path with a man friend. We were stopped by an enormous serpent rolled into a ball as high as my shoulder, blocking the way. It was so threatening that we thought of pushing it off the path with a long pole.*

I was walking with an animus figure. The serpent ball shows a real block, a trauma at a deep instinctual level, since a serpent can symbolize the Earth Mother, she who rules the animal world of the instincts. I felt the serpent sphere represented my mother complex, or my unconscious, undigested fear of all mothers and women in general. With help from the animus, I could better cope with the serpent.

> *Four months later I dreamt I was alone and I again met a large sphere of many entwined serpents blocking the way. On top of the serpent ball lay a black dog asleep. (The dog belonged to an older woman friend, a mother type.) I was not afraid of the serpents because of the unharmed dog, so I passed by.*

Because of the unharmed dog my fear was allayed. The dog is a protective symbol of loyalty and instinctive trust. This symbol of instinctual life is in the dream at a higher level than the serpent. That it is black and asleep tells me that I must awaken the dog in me to help control the many aspects of serpent energy it is lying on. This ultimately led to the idea, dreamt a year later, that the serpent power might become conscious in a new way. In the symbolism of the next dream, the serpent becomes ennobled.

> *I was with the daughter of a friend. Her mother in real life had been a Russian princess. In the dream she told me that she had lost the papers that proved her title. "They are hidden in a box in the earth," I said. Digging beneath the earth I found a square black box and within it were her lost papers. Out of a small hole next to where the box had been there came a tiny serpent. It looked at us and we saw that on its head was a minute golden crown. I said, "He is the royal guardian of the box."*

> *In another dream a few months later I was gathering snake venom with a woman friend to use in a positive way.*

The first dream was a very important one for me. The young princess symbolized a rejuvenated form of the spiritual universal mother figure. As a new aspect of myself, she needed proof of her identity, the essence of her femininity, which I found by digging into mother earth and opening up an archetypal aspect of the mother to the light of day. The serpent energy accordingly was transformed, appearing as a crowned serpent, an inner manifestation of the Self. I recognized this by saying, "It is the royal guardian of the box."

In the second dream, with my shadow counterpart, a woman friend, I gathered serpent venom to use positively. I was taking on the responsibility for transforming the dark side of my nature —venom—into something positive.

But the undulating snake line on the Stone was also a river. I have had several dreams of crossing a river, and even of going through a tunnel under a river to the other side. This usually symbolizes a step forward in one's inner development, or the crossing of the great river of life to the other side. The river moves, flows in time from its mountain source into the ocean of the unconscious.

With my eyes still closed, I pictured the Stone's mandala face very clearly in my mind. Hermes, with Mercury on his tunic, was between the Sun and the Moon and four other planetary symbols, making seven archetypal images. I knew that I must look on them with great care and be constantly aware that their message for me, a woman, is different from what they symbolize for Jung, a man. It was also possible that some of these symbols wouldn't speak to me at all.

Collectively, they are "The Sacred Seven of the Heavenly Bodies," the inspiration for countless myths and gods that man has worshipped as a close family. In my research I had found an even more interesting fact: All these gods have in some way been worshipped as, or connected with, stones. Kronos-Saturn was fated to be overcome by Zeus-Jupiter; he was tricked into swallowing a stone wrapped in swaddling clothes that he thought was his son. Zeus-Jupiter was worshipped in the form of a stone that was used in the taking of oaths, as we use the Bible. Aphrodite-Venus was worshipped in the form of a *dorm* or a conical stone, either black or white in color, showing the negative and positive sides of her nature. Ares-Mars was knocked down by a stone thrown by Athena-Minerva during the battle of the gods. Hermes-Mercury was also worshipped as a *herm*, a carved stone placed on roads to protect the traveler. The Sun-god, Mithra, was born from a stone and the earliest representation of the moon in the form of a cone.

Wondering what my next step forward would be, I said to Hermes, standing in his circle, "I count on you to point out what these special planetary symbols hold for me." Hermes seemed to move his lantern up and down in assent, and I, meditating on the Stone itself, took note again that it was a complete cube; whereupon, as if in answer to my close regard, it gradually darkened until all of Jung's carvings were obliterated. I thought of T. S. Eliot: "And any action is a step to the block, to the fire, down the sea's throat. Or to an illegible stone; and that is where we start."

I suddenly realized that the dark cube resembled the black box of my dream that the crowned serpent was guarding! Looking more closely, I noticed that in the center of what had been the mandala face of the Stone, a dial was appearing. It seemed to replace Hermes' circle. There was no doubt about it—the Stone had turned into a black treasure box. As the dial lightened, I saw Hermes' symbol in its center. This told me that, with the aid of Hermes, the necessary combination to open the box would be given to me. My challenge then would be to become aware of what the Stone had to give to me, a woman.

As if in answer to my inner thoughts, a light, the light from Hermes' lantern, left the dial and lit up the symbol of the sun. I knew then that Hermes was lighting my Way, so I asked myself a question: "What is the sun to me?"

Being an early-morning riser, I am very conscious of the sun's daily journey. Often I watch the first streak of sacred light that announces his coming. There is complete silence; all of nature, including myself, seems to hold its breath awaiting the sun's birth and the dispelling of darkness. Next comes the music of the birds to herald his arrival. The sun god is born, and all of nature rejoices and is aware of his life-giving powers—his march up, up into the sky, and a fullness that can heal and product growth, and also the fire-heat that can burn and destroy. As the sun terminates his day journey, he creates ever-changing sunsets, especially at Big Sur, where golden light, fiery red light, becomes a part of the sky. The sun himself assumes odd shapes and casts strange reflections, as he slowly sinks into the ocean—the underworld of man, to vanquish the powers of darkness and evil.

This mysterious journey was an inspiration and source of countless myths, symbolic journeys toward ritual death and rebirth into the wholeness of man. No wonder the sun symbolizes the active male principle of the universe, the Logos, and the material aspect of God the Father.

I must not forget, either, that in astrology the sun is the sphere that influences its related zodiacal sign, Leo. In my horoscope, Leo is the rising sign. Jung himself was a Leo, and this is another reason I felt so strong an affinity for him and the Stone. As I gazed on the sun circle, I said, "You are the One, the All, the center of our solar system. As a symbol of unity you are the Self."

The light from Hermes' lantern seemed to move from the sun to the other side of the dial, and rested on the moon. I knew she was the sun's opposite and symbolized the passive feminine principle of the universe, and Eros. On the Stone she is the waning moon, who rules and controls the negative and mysterious forces of her domain, the Underworld. In repeating her monthly cycles from birth to death, she rules the great rhythms of Nature and life and, in a way, time.

The moon is extremely important to me, but not in a romantic way anymore, especially since man has walked on her surface, leaving behind him his debris. From childhood, I have been very much aware of her presence in the night sky—not because I am a woman, or because I plant my vegetable seeds by the moon's phases, or because she is a mother-figure, but because I am conscious of her compelling, almost dangerous, psychic forces.

Gazing on her symbol, I felt that I could reach out and grab the moon's tip with my hand the way I would grasp a sickle or scythe. This reminded me of the terrifying dream I once had of killing the evil mother-figure with a moon-shaped sword. Imagining the scythe in my hand, I now felt that it must not be used to kill, but to cut away the old part of myself, to make way for the new selfhood to come.

Her psychic forces had certainly held sway over me in a frightening experience I had had many years before when living alone with the Mam Indians of Todos Santos in Guatemala. One night I had gone outside my little hut to gaze on the full moon.

The sleeping village lay below me; above the towering mountains opposite hung the immense orb of the moon. Silence prevailed except for an occasional cry of coyotes, or a distant bark of a dog.

Feeling sad and lonely as I gazed in a sort of trance on the hypnotic moon, I suddenly felt myself mount upward, leaving my body where I had been sitting. Looking down on it, I was more than frightened, and prayed for help. My prayer was answered, for I found myself again in my body, walking into my hut. I felt so peculiar and apprehensive that I bent down and splashed my face in the bucket of cold water that was my wash basin. To my horror, my hand encountered a dead mouse. This gave me the jolt I needed to feel again that I was a normal human being with my feet on the ground.

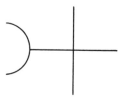

I returned my meditative thoughts to the Stone. As the moon symbol faded into darkness, Jupiter's symbol slowly appeared to the left of the dial, next to where I had seen the sun. This sign, made up of the cross of earth and the new moon, symbolized for me a different birth, a spiritual birth on this earth. In mythology, Jupiter was the Father of the Gods and ruled insight into the mystery of life. For me he also symbolized my own personal father, who had had many of the attributes of Jupiter, such as intelligence, will, and justice. For me Jupiter also represented Jung, Dr. L., and all medicine men and shamans who have insight into the veiled mysteries of Life.

Then, as I looked, the Stone darkened again, and to the right of the dial emerged the illuminated symbol of Venus. It consisted of the moon's sphere with the earth sign below. The full moon above the firmament, I thought. I knew she symbolized generation, fertility, and Eros, but I thought of her more as a goddess of love, beauty, and the arts. I saw her as Botticelli painted her, standing in a fluted shell. She was the virgin born from the foam of the sea, the essence of grace and all that is lovely and gentle. Venus was also an initiating goddess of the mysteries, and as the soul-temptress of man she was an enchanting, seducing, orgiastic woman. Venus is an important symbol for me. She stands for much of what was left out of my earlier sense of identity.

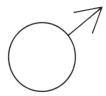

The box turned completely black again except for the central dial. Looking beneath the dial, I awaited the coming of Mars. He did not appear, and I wondered why he had not been illuminated by Hermes' lantern. Was Hermes playing a game with me? As if in answer to my unspoken question, I realized that Mars had little to say to me—he was not for me. I remembered he was the god of war and fire and the power and energy of life—the power to destroy so as to create. He had many negative qualities that his family well describe: when Mars went into battle, his sisters, Strife, and his sons, Terror, went with him.

Gazing on the dark treasure box I saw the symbol of Saturn, a cross with the new moon, appearing above the dial. Although I knew he was god of time and life and death and earth as the sower of the seed, I thought of him more as the guardian of the treasure, with his servants, the gnomes. Also, Jung had hinted that in some way he was connected to Mercury, so I must like him and accept him for what he was for me, even though he was a grim god, giving off a feeling of coldness and dryness.

The treasure box turned completely black again, and out of the darkness emerged the mandala face with Hermes at the center point. I felt strongly that something had been left out, and guessed that it was the alchemical aspect of the symbols. Not knowing much about alchemy, I wondered what I had not seen that it was necessary to know about in relation to the Stone and myself. I had read that Saturn was called *Mercurius Senex* by the alchemists, maybe because his metal was lead, which was thought of as the *prima materia*. My eyes rested on the sun and moon symbols. I remembered that together they symbolize Logos and Eros and the King and Queen. Just as I must bring my opposite natures together, the great work of the alchemists was a bringing together, a *coniunctio*, a marriage of the sun and moon within the alchemical vessel, to find their gold, a symbol of the Philosophers' Stone.

But Hermes spoke again. "Tell me more about the research you have done on me," he said, encouragingly.

"In Arcadian Greece," I answered, "you were first a spirit that occupied either a pile of stones found on pathways and in front of houses, or an uncarved stone-shaped shaft. These were signposts to aid travelers on their way. Then you became a *herm*, a square pillar of carved stone topped by your head, and half-way down the shaft was your erect phallus. In this form you were worshipped as a fertility god. So way back in Grecian times, you were the spirit of stones."

"But my beginnings as projected by man into time sink way back in history. I was not always connected with stones," Hermes said. "Around 2,500 B.C. I was worshipped in Mesopotamia and Egypt. In Mesopotamia I was Ninshubar, chief messenger of the gods. I held a magic wand or rod then, as I do now. It was a phallic and fertility symbol. In Egypt I became the god Thoth and was exceedingly wise. As the scribe of the gods I had an Ibis head, and I judged the dead by weighing their hearts against the feather of truth. Later I was identified with the moon. Sometimes I was identified with an ape."

"I have seen you as Thoth," I said, "in wall paintings in Egyptian tombs. In fact, I own a small Egyptian stone statue of you." I thought this would please him.

Without changing, he continued, "As the moon-crowned Thoth, I was considered to be a magician and later became identified with your Satan. In Hellenistic times I became Hermes Trismagistus, Thrice Greatest Hermes, identified with all the esoteric sciences. I was the author of many books, one called

The Book of Thoth, which was also named *The Devil's Book*. My greatest achievement in the field of alchemy was as the author of the 'Emerald Tablet' or 'Tabula Smaragdina.' That book was a great influence on the alchemists of the Middle Ages."

"Jung quotes frequently from your book," I said, feeling that I was on the threshold of a new insight. "I recall one passage about a symbolic sun-moon child, where it says:

> Its father is the sun, its mother the moon; the wind hath carried it in his belly; its nurse is the earth. Its power is complete when it is turned towards the earth. It ascendeth from the earth to heaven, and descendeth again to the earth, and receiveth the power of the higher and lower things. So wilt thou have the glory of the whole world.

Jung says of this passage, "As the 'Tabula Smaragdina' shows, the purpose of the ascent and descent of the sun-moon child through the planetary spheres, is to unite the powers of Above and Below."[1]

"The Greeks," I continued, "saw you as the great messenger of the gods, with your winged hat and sandals. You carried your magic rod, which often was crowned with three leaves. It was said to have been given to you by Apollo to be your herald's staff, and in time it turned into the caduceus, with two entwined copulating serpents symbolizing the serpent energy and union of the opposites. In India the wand symbolized the axis of the world, and the two serpents, the energy of Kundalini. Today the same caduceus is a symbol of medicine and also of transportation, since you were also the god of commerce. With this rod you became the mediator between the two worlds, an initiator into the sacred mysteries and secret lore. You closed the eyes of the dying, led the souls of those who had died into the underworld, and also conducted the souls to be reborn. In this role, you were regarded as the generator both of new lives and of new life!

"Don't think that I am unaware of your dark side, however," I went on. "Everyone has one, even gods. You were always known as a trickster, a liar, and a cheat. You loved intrigue; you were lustful and far from moral. I must be careful not to call on your dark aspects—not that I, myself, would mind being a bit immoral now and then."

Hermes answered in his own defense: "You must not forget

that, besides having a dark side and a light, I am androgyne, male and female, and am known for uniting them within myself."

"Yes," I answered, "and I recall Jung said in one of his essays on mythology: 'It is a remarkable fact that perhaps the majority of cosmogonic gods are of a bisexual nature. The hermaphrodite means nothing but a union of the strongest and most striking opposites.' "[2]

"When I first saw you at Bollingen, I immediately noticed the sign of Mercury on your body, combining the crescent moon, the Sun, and below, the cross, the symbol of earth. In my horoscope, you are my planet, since my sun sign is Gemini, the twins. This might be another reason that I am attracted to you and your dual nature. The alchemists, too, took you as the ideal symbol of their mysterious transforming substance, quicksilver, to which they gave your name *Mercurius*, for, like you, quicksilver had the power to unite the opposites within itself, being both solid and fluid. Yes, I remember that Jung said: '. . . The double nature of *Mercurius*, which shows itself . . . in the Uroborus, the dragon that devours, fertilizes, begets, and slays itself and brings itself to life again.'[3] You personify many, many different opposites: water and fire, earth and air, square and round, matter and the Philosophers' Stone, and many more. You were considered to be the alchemist's inspiration, but also his ruin. The alchemists often said that 'the *opus* proceeds from the one and leads back to the one, . . . a sort of circle like a dragon biting his own tail.'[4] And one of the basic symbols of alchemy, this serpent, the Uroborus, is your symbol as well as the great transformer."

"That is all very true," agreed Hermes. "You have learned your lesson well. But there is more to me than what is revealed in books. The time has come for you to experience me inwardly as you search for your treasure, especially since I am a guard to secret places. As you continue on your way, you will notice that the messages and symbols on the Stone will be continually changing; if you pay attention to the changes, each change will open to you a new context."

"Yes! I realize this," I told him, "and I am counting on you, with your dual nature and your willingness, to help me unravel all these messages and symbols—from my own point of view, that of a woman."

I waited, but no answer came. Mercury, as I should have known, was not one to bind himself with promises. I hoped that with luck, he would still be with me, and the images of my imagination would be transmuted into personal inner experiences. The interweaving of my fantasy and the meanings of the symbols would then work in its own way.

CHAPTER IX

The Kingdom of the Child

After the conversations with Hermes, I was convinced that a most difficult challenge still lay ahead of me on my path of initiation. Was I able to face the mystery of the unknown? This question made me wonder what assets I had to enable me to assimilate the enigmatic messages on Jung's Stone. Because of my analysis, I now had much more confidence in myself, especially with Hermes serving as guide to conduct me into his world. I was confident that he could also show me a new way of looking at things long familiar to me that would now take on new meanings.

Realizing that I was not so clever as I had thought, nor endowed with very great intellectual powers, I was nonetheless convinced that I had some qualifications: maybe just that I was an ordinary human being, open to receive what came my way with gratitude and humility, and that I now knew myself somewhat and felt an inner steadfastness that I could count on. It came to me that I must regard the Stone's messages as clues to be used only if they spoke to me. In my new relationship to Hermes, I knew I must be constantly aware of the danger of becoming too closely identified with him. I must not allow that to happen, I thought, or he will possess me.

At the same time I had begun to understand the position of my ego in relation to the Self. I saw those two as two telephone operators: the Self, chief operator in the inner world, and the ego, an operator in the outer world. When the Self plugged in a hot line to my ego, it would be up to the ego, as the center of consciousness, to control, to balance, and to judge whether to allow the call to come through. This the ego could do only if it realized that it is not altogether in charge, that the Self is the chief functioning authority.

I had learned that the first written message that Jung carved on the uncut Stone had come to him when he first had gazed on it. Here are the words, translated from Latin, as given in his autobiography:

> Here stands the mean, uncomely stone,
> 'Tis very cheap in price!
> The more it is despised by fools,
> The more loved by the wise.[1]

This verse had come from a well-known alchemist-astrologer and physician of the thirteenth century, Arnaldus de Villanova, and refers to the Stone of the wise, the *lapis*.

I thought of the Bible and the verse found in Psalm 118:22:

> The Stone which the builders rejected
> has become the head of the corner.
> This is the Lord's doing;
> it is marvelous in our eyes.

Another similar reference applies to the concept of the Tao:

> The "Cornerstone, who makes both one" is a particularly interesting symbol of the divine as the "reconciling principle" in which the "pairs of opposites" are transcended. The symbol is widespread, and is found in China as the *tai ch'i*, the Great Ultimate . . . underlying and uniting *yang* and *yin*.[2]

> Tao is eternal, but has no fame (name);
> The Uncarved Block, though seemingly of small account,
> Is greater than anything that is under heaven.[3]

Jung once told me that the mandala that he carved on the Stone was the eye of a fish and that in the small circle one can see his own reflection. In his autobiography Jung says:

> I began to see on the front face . . . a small circle, a sort of eye, which looked at me. I chiseled it into the stone, and in the center made a tiny homunculus. This corresponds to the "little doll" *(pupilla)*—yourself—which you see in the pupil of another's eye; a kind of Kabir, or the Telesphorus of Asklepios.[4]

On the same central face of the Stone he had chiseled a second message in Greek:

Time is a child—playing like a child—playing a board game—
the kingdom of the child. This is Telesphorus, who roams
through the dark regions of this cosmos and glows like a star
out of the depths. He points the way to the gates of the sun
and the land of dreams.

Time is a child! "That describes you," I said to my little guide,
and the words of T. S. Eliot opened to me their meaning:

Time present and time past
Are both perhaps present in time future,
And time future contained in time past.
If all time is eternally present
All time is unredeemable.
What might have been is an abstraction
Remaining a perpetual possibility
Only in a world of speculation.
What might have been and what has been
Point to one end, which is always present. . . .

Words move, music moves
Only in time; but that which is only living
Can only die. Words, after speech, reach
Into the silence. Only by the form, the pattern,
Can words or music reach
The stillness, as a Chinese jar still
Moves perpetually in its stillness.
Not the stillness of the violin, while the note lasts,
Not that only, but the co-existence,
Or say that the end precedes the beginning,
And the end and the beginning were always there
Before the beginning and after the end.
And all is always now. . . .[5]

Of course, I had often considered the question of time, but
my concept had been rather abstract. I realized that material
objects like clocks, radios, televisions, and calendars govern our
lives in time and that these, in turn, are governed by *sidereal*
time. But there are periods also of *psychological* time. There is
the question of *cyclical* versus *consecutive* time. The world and
time must have been born simultaneously. In relation to time,
Jung put forward the idea of *synchronicity*, a concept that I considered when, directly after my dream of a turtle, I met the live
turtle. Somewhere I have read that "what Jung calls synchronistic

events are in fact something like 'acts of creation in time.'"[6] When I lived with the Indians, time seemed not to exist. It had no importance. I was part of nature, one with nature, and so experienced still another type of time: *eternal* time, eternity that has no beginning nor end.

Does time flow forward or backward? Is it a straight line or a circle, like the circular serpent with its tail in its mouth that symbolizes eternity and eternal rebirth? Time might even be a moving spiral that rolls into a central source, like the inner circle of the Stone, and then rolls out again. Perhaps such an inner source could be compared to the world of the Self and the fourth dimension, the outer circle then being compared to our three-dimensional world.

I realized that I was more attuned to immediate time than to either past or future. I did not live in the past or worry much about the future, and when I meditated I went out of time into a sort of experienced timelessness. Then even my breath seemed not to be contained or constrained by my body. Breathing became a descent within myself and yet beyond myself into the cosmos.

In playing with these ideas, I pictured Hermes in the center of the Stone, in his circle. I even envisioned him inviting me in. He would seem to beckon to me, saying, "Won't you come into my parlor?" like the well known spider to the fly.

"You do in a way resemble a spider in the center of its web," I would say. "And yes, I will accept your invitation, knowing well that you are not the evil black widow that has been appearing in my dreams."

For over four years, I had been having occasional dreams of fearful, deadly black widow spiders. Not only did I dream of them, but I also found them alive, both outside and inside my house at Big Sur. My fear of them lessened when I made a detailed drawing of one that I had killed with DDT. What a wonderful symbol that was of my mother complex! In the first dream such a spider bit my hand; in the second, she attached her thread to my bed; in the third, a man friend killed a male and a female black widow directly under my bed; whereas my last spider dream was of an initiation scene. The spider, I already knew, was associated with the moon and the phenomenal world of the senses, as well as with death and rebirth. Its web is seen as a spiral leading to the central point where it sits, like Hermes in his mandala. Again considering Hermes in his circle, I was now amazed to see that he had vanished and that in his place there stood a goddess, the beautiful Hindu goddess Maya, eternal weaver of the web of illusion, creator of the world and of space and form. "Just as the spider pours forth its thread from itself and takes it back again . . . even so the universe grows from the Imperishable."[7]

But now the circle within which Maya stood became empty and resembled the unmoving hub of a wheel around which the large circle, the wheel of time, was turning. I thought of the Tibetan Wheel of Life, the potter's wheel, and the spinning wheel, all symbolizing the circle of the universe; also the sacred wheel of the *I Ching*, the wheel of the zodiac, a water wheel, the alchemist's wheel, Ezekiel's fiery wheel, a *chakra*, the wheel of Vishnu, the Buddhist Wheel of the Law which can never be turned backwards, and finally the wheel of the Stone. They all turned from east to west, from birth to death, to be reborn.

When the child Hermes appeared again within his circle, I wondered if it were a doorway that might lead into the circle of eternity, the circle of emptiness of Chinese philosophy. The circle of eternity and the unmoving hub of the wheel are similar to the unmoved mover of time in its universal sense. And the circular movement of the circumference of the wheel corresponds to the weaving of the spider and the fashioning and destruction of the world, which suggests a worldly sense of time that certainly is not of eternal time.

So the wheel of time turns, and the center, the hub, is motionless; it is timeless; it is eternal, the living world where the opposites do not exist, nor is there time nor space. Is the child archetype within the hub of the wheel of time a creator—timeless, invisible, and eternal, like the Goddess Maya and the spider? If so, he is also his own visible creation, a projection into time and space, like the web of illusion, the moving circumference of the wheel, and the large circle of the Stone.

Rilke wrote:

O hours of childhood,
hours when behind the figures there was more
than the mere past, and when what lay before us
was not the future! True, we were growing, and sometimes

made haste to be grown up, half for the sake
of those who'd nothing left but their grown-upness.
Yet, when alone, we entertained ourselves
within everlastingness: there we would stand,
within the gap left between world and toy,
upon a spot which, from the first beginning,
had been established for a pure event.[8]

"Time is a child—playing like a child—playing a board game
—the kingdom of the child."

If we could return to our childhood and play a game on a
board, like Alice on the chessboard in her special world, could
we too become queens who first were pawns? As a child I used
to play by the hour either with Jerome or with a next-door neighbor who had a donkey that he named after me. We made toys
out of odd pieces of wood, stones, or anything that resembled
what we sought. And in a hidden, unused part of the garden,
Romie and I played our favorite secret game. We created our own
country made up of rolling hills, mountains, and even lakes made
of mirrors. We planted twigs for trees and laid paths. In strategic
places we put magic people with flowing robes, hollyhock people
in red, white, and pink. The next morning we could hardly wait
to rush out to the garden to see if our special country had been
visited during the night. If anything had moved, we knew that
fairy beings had called on us.

In my adult world, the act of "play" remains a positive thing. I
play when I work in my vegetable garden, loving my plants and
talking to them, imagining that weeds and harmful insects are
the enemy and that I am saving the plants from being annihi-
lated. When I cook, paint, or write, these also are forms of play,
and I am unconscious, oblivious of what is around me. Psychologically, I am unable to "play" if there is any struggle or strife between my ego and the Self.

There is something pure and exceedingly wise about a young
child, as if he were in touch with something with which we have
lost contact. The Taoists feel that an infant is nearest of all to
Tao. Is it because a young child's ego has not yet been born into
consciousness and he is still very close to his collective unconscious and eternity? So the Child on the Stone stands in a doorway that leads both in and out. He stands between his two

worlds, the inner and outer, the invisible and the visible, heaven and earth.

To "play like a child" would be a pure creative act, creation from within. Jung admitted that he played like a child when he carved the Stone, manifesting whatever arose from a timeless creative source. "I also play like a child when I play with you," I said to Hermes.

If the archetypal Child is on the threshold between the two sides of nature, then that threshold itself is a bridge joining two worlds. When the Child passes over the bridge into his inner world, his creative world, he is out of time and space and experiencing eternity, *eternal time*. But as soon as he "plays a game on a board," he recrosses the bridge into his outer world and manifests himself in time and space, in *sidereal time* and the world of opposites. When he is in the middle of the bridge, he is in perfect balance; for he is then bridging his two worlds of eternal time and sidereal time. At such a moment he experiences the wholeness of time—the timelessness of time, and the "now." Time is a child.

"Time is a child—playing like a child—playing a board game —the kingdom of the child."

"The kingdom of the child" is explained by Jung when he says:

> In analysis the path leads to the "land of childhood," the time before the rational present-day consciousness separated from the historical psyche, the collective unconscious; not only to the land where the complexes of childhood have their origin, but to a prehistoric country which was the cradle of all our psyches.[9]

The board might be likened to the quaternity, the archetype of the "special child," and from the alchemist's point of view the child is Mercury-Hermes. Playing a game on a board could represent the interaction of the opposites and also the mystical union of the four elements that concerned the alchemist, or the squaring of the circle. Mercury is "he who succeeds in bringing about the squaring of the circle, who represents the mystery and the solution." The squaring of the circle is an ancient expression that means manifesting wholeness, or the totality of the four elements. From a psychological point of view, my wholeness will be attained when I gain conscious control of *all* of my functions, except my inferior function. This can be included in consciousness, but is never under conscious control.

All of this is on the Stone—the square, the circle, the four divisions, and Hermes, standing at the mid-point. Hermes is the secret and at the same time its solution.

The next clue to the inner meaning of the Child lies in the inscription: "This is Telesphorus, who roams through the dark regions of this cosmos and glows like a star out of the depths. He points the way to the gates of the sun, and the land of dreams."

In Jung's autobiography he speaks of a manikin that he carved at the age of ten. I suspect it was the prototype of the Child of the Stone. "The manikin was a little cloaked god of the ancient world, a Telesphorus such as stands on monuments of Asklepios and reads to him from a scroll."[10] Jung placed the carving and an "oblong blackish stone" in a pencil box. He felt that the stone was the manikin's stone and that it was all very secret, so he hid the box on one of the beams under the roof, "for no one must see it."

Shutting my eyes, I said to Hermes, "I know that you are also Telesphorus, for both you and Jung have told me this, yet I can't help but be amazed at all the facets of your nature that I have discovered in my research. *Opposites* seems to be the key word to your contrary nature; this is understandable, since you are half male and half female. As Telesphorus, you contain within yourself the power to oscillate from one extreme to another and to synthesize these opposites into wholeness. You were the Greek God of the physicians, a healer who made whole. You belonged to the cult of Asclepius, in which the ritual of incubation was used. You were represented there as both an old man and a boy who brought fulfillment of dreams and prayers, and in this aspect you were named 'He that Brings Things to an End.'

"You were also called 'The Begetter and the Begotten,' and as such were associated with the phallus as a symbol of psychic energy in its creative aspect. And in this character you were connected with the Cabiri, who had a phallic aspect. Their cone-shaped hoods, similar to yours, are related to the Phrygian cap that had the power to make the wearer invisible. The last line on the central face of the Stone is a quotation from Homer: 'He points the way to the Gates of the Sun.'"

On the wheel of the zodiac, the Gates of the Sun were the signs for Cancer, a water sign, and Capricorn, an earth sign, which were opposites, and the two solstices were placed in these signs. Picturing the mandala-like face of the Stone, I can imagine that the large circle is a zodiacal wheel with its twelve signs; to his right, where Hermes is pointing, is where Cancer would be. Esoterically this would be the west, where the sun sinks and dies: the entrance to Hermes' world, the unconscious, the "Land of Dreams." Capricorn is opposite Cancer on the wheel: the east, where the sun seemingly rises out of the earth and man is re-born into consciousness. In his left hand, the past, is a lantern to light the way, or to bring the light of understanding into the un-conscious as he did on the black box, so he really points the way into the unconscious and the way out not only for me, but for all who notice him. It is the way of the sun behind the earth, from west to east, from death to rebirth. This west-east movement was used by the Indians I worked with, and all primitive people, to contact psychic powers. In my view this movement is connected again with the wheel, a well known symbol in alchemy, which represents circulation and distillation, so necessary for alchem-ical work. In fact, the alchemists' work or opus was called *Rota* (wheel). That the sun is on Hermes' right indicates a downward male cycle and the moon to the left an upward female cycle. The movements associated with the sun and moon, the rising and setting, the waxing and waning, indicate the in and out move-ment of psychic energy and of Hermes, my guide.

"As I look at you, Hermes," I said, "standing in your circle, you give me the feeling of expansion and contraction. It would not surprise me at all if you grew into a giant or shrank into the size of Tom Thumb. As Hermes, you are a Divine Child with a miraculous birth that corresponds to psychic birth."

Jung points out that a child's birth rises out of the depths of nature, the depth of the unconscious. This is symbolic of forces beyond our conscious comprehension, though intuitively we sense it tells us that this birth is symbolic of the deep desire for self-realization and wholeness.

Jung has pointed to all the trials that the child-hero has to go through; how tiny he is, how alone and unprotected from the many dangers and difficulties that beset him. However, though these dangers seem insurmountable, the child-hero has inherent within himself what he needs, the power of the gods, which carries him through all obstacles.

"Also," I said to Hermes, "I must not forget to look on you as just an ordinary child, symbolic of my own childhood, of the times when I was contained and happy and the times when I felt rejected, unloved, and misunderstood."

I had had many dreams of babies. The following seven dreams took place during a period of seven years. The first occurred a year after I had commenced my analysis. I feel that these dreams speak for themselves and need no interpretation.

A voice said, "Poor murdered little girl." I was on a desert pulling a couch on wheels. On it lay a woman friend (a shadow figure). I pulled her off and underneath I found my mother.

A woman friend (also a shadow figure) gave birth to a baby. I washed my hands, broke the umbilical cord, as I had no knife, and knotted it, then covered the mother and babe with a blanket.

I was carrying my baby on my back, like an Indian.

People told me that my cousin's baby had died—choked on mucous. I unwrapped the tiny baby and laid it in my left hand to warm it. I put my mouth to its mouth and breathed in and out to a count of four. It commenced to move, so I told the people to give it warm milk from a medicine dropper.

I was in an old house with a woman friend. We felt that a sin had been committed by an elderly woman and her maid—owners of the house. We found hidden in a big chest a small square box and in it a dead, dried-up baby with its clothes and birth documents. We knew that the baby had been killed—smothered. This was the sin.

I was climbing a ladder with a man friend, my animus. A man's voice from above said, "Be as a little child."

A woman my age was about to give birth to a baby. I told her I would take care of things. It was born and I helped her cut the cord and then I wrapped the baby in a blanket. It was a baby boy.

Not only do these dreams point to some early childhood trauma in my relationship with my mother, but they also show how a person in analysis inevitably goes back to the origin of things, to when there was an original sensed unity with all life. This condition has always been represented by the figure of a hermaphroditic being, living, as it were, before there was any differentiation into the opposites, male-female, man-woman, father-mother. When Jung talks of the hermaphroditic aspect of the child, he says:

> As civilization develops, the bisexual "primary being" turns into a symbol of the unity of the personality, a symbol of the *self* where the war of opposites finds peace. In this way the primary being becomes the distant *goal* of man's self-development, having been from the very beginning a projection of unconscious wholeness.[11]

"You are not only standing in the center of your circle," I now said to Hermes, resuming our conversation, "but you are also the center of a cross, a St. Andrew's cross, called the cross of the Martyrdom of Man and also the cross of perfection. It has the force to synthesize the upper and lower worlds. It is the sign for the number ten, which symbolizes completion, and is also a sign for multiplication. In this contest you, Hermes, symbolize for me Plato's world-soul crucified in space, or man suspended between the opposites."

Jung says of the hero:

> The cross, or whatever other heavy burden the hero carries, is *himself*, or rather *the* self, his wholeness, which is both God and animal—not merely the empirical man, but the totality of his being, which is rooted in his animal nature and reaches out beyond the merely human towards the divine.[12]

To the Chinese, "the upper and lower halves of the diagonal cross in the old form of *wu* (the character for five) . . . constitute two triangles, one pointing down, the other up. . . . In terms of the Elements, the two triangles stood for the Element of Fire . . . (Yang Principle) and that of Water . . . (Yin Principle)."[13]

I see also another cross on the Stone that is less visible: the cardinal cross called the Cross of the Gods, which is an ancient symbol of generation. The vertical male line is formed by Mars, Hermes, and Saturn; the horizontal female line by the Sun, Jupiter, Hermes, Venus, and the Moon. The horizontal line is female and passive, the vertical line is male and active. This cross symbolizes synthesis of the opposites or wholeness, just as Hermes does.

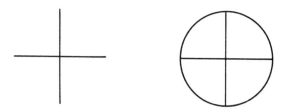

Encircled, it is the sun cross of Wotan and a symbol of the human soul.

"Hermes," I said, "as the point where the cross intersects, you are the One; and as manifest to the ends of the cross, you are the All. As you and I know, the cross has been found all over the world since primordial times. Everywhere it is a sacred and religious symbol that stands for the mystery of life. It was associated with wisdom and fertility and with the four winds and the four quarters of the earth, thus it symbolizes earth." To the Indians of the Americas the cross is a well known religious symbol that was used by them long before the Spaniards brought the Christian cross to the Americas.

I see the cross as a tree with one end buried in the unconscious and the other stretching upward into the limitless sky of the gods and of consciousness. I associate this tree with the cross of Christ's suffering, his crucifixion, his descent into hell to conquer death, and his resurrection. So the cross with its horizontal and vertical lines, female and male, is to me symbolic of suffering and death for rebirth—death of the old personality for psychic rebirth.

There is one more great theme to be associated with the cross. While I was working with the Navaho, I was invited to my first ceremony. During the making of the sand painting, the medicine man asked me a question. "What is the most important thing in the world?" Luckily I did not have time to think. My answer was, "A heart." He said, "Yes, the Navaho had a heart until the white man taught him otherwise."

The New Testament says, "For where your treasure is, there will your heart be also." (Luke 12:34) I was brought up to believe that God is love and love is God. Yet do I know what love is? "Love thy neighbor as thyself." What does that mean? How can I love my neighbor as myself when I am not sure whether I love myself or if I am even capable of loving myself?

Jung says of love:

> I sometimes feel that Paul's words—"Though I speak with the tongues of men and of angels, and have not love"—might well be the first condition of all cognition and the quintessence of divinity itself. . . . In my medical experience as well as in my own life I have again and again been faced with the mystery of love, and have never been able to explain what it is. . . . Love "bears all things" and "endures all things" (I Cor. 13:7). These words say all there is to be said; nothing can be added to them.[14]

There are two kinds of love, human and divine. Human love entails the complete giving of oneself to another being, the love that a mother gives to her child, or the love between two lovers. I feel that the need that motivates this giving is the desire for wholeness. Christ's complete surrender on the cross is symbolic of divine love and its earthly counterpart, the giving over of oneself utterly to God in the way, for example, of a novitiate monk surrendering himself to divinity.

In the initiation rites there is always a symbolic death or sacrifice involving complete surrender of the old personality, the giving over of the ego as director of the psyche to serve under the real director, the Self, which is identical with that spirit within me which I could just as well name God or Love. The child Hermes, as this Self, would be Love, the "One" that embraces the all,

114 THE STONE SPEAKS

or Christ, or Buddha. And this Spirit not only is within, it is also outside of time and space, for it is eternal.

What I now had come to realize was that if it were possible for me to discover and experience the Self, then—and only then —would I be capable of knowing and loving myself, which would be tantamount to knowing and loving God and my neighbor as myself.

The alchemists looked on the Stone as an inner experience of the Self, or God. I wonder if Jung felt the same way about his Stone as he carved it.

One Two Three Four

I now knew that my next confrontation was to be with the uniquely enigmatic formula that Jung gave to me when he explained the four radiating lines on the Stone. "You see," he said, "four divisions into four-four parts: here are three lightnings and one river. Three were supposed to be equal and one had a double meaning and that's the one here, the river, and this is an old alchemist secret, the so-called Axioma Maria. This has played a very great role through seventeen hundred years of alchemy."

I realized that if I were even to attempt to guess the formula's meaning, I would have to try to understand at least a bit of what alchemy meant to Jung. In his autobiography he says:

> I had very soon seen that analytical psychology coincided in a most curious way with alchemy. . . . This was, of course, a momentous discovery: I had stumbled upon the historical counterpart of my psychology of the unconscious. . . . When I pored over these old texts everything fell into place: the fantasy-images, the empirical material I had gathered in my practice, and the conclusions I had drawn from it. I now began to understand what these psychic contents meant when seen in historical perspective. . . . The primordial images and the nature of the archetype took a central place in my researches, and it became clear to me that without history there can be no psychology, and certainly no psychology of the unconscious. A psychology of consciousness can, to be sure, content itself with material drawn from personal life.[1]

In *Psychology and Alchemy*, Jung says more:

> The point is that alchemy is rather like an undercurrent to the
> Christianity that ruled on the surface. It is to this surface as the
> dream is to consciousness, and just as the dream compensates
> the conflicts of the conscious mind, so alchemy endeavors to fill
> in the gaps left by the Christian tension of opposites. Perhaps
> the most pregnant expression of this is the axiom of Maria Pro-
> phetissa . . . which runs like a leitmotif throughout almost the
> whole of the lifetime of alchemy, extending over more than sev-
> enteen centuries.[2]

The saying of Maria Prophetissa is: "One becomes two, two
becomes three, and out of the third comes the one as the fourth."
When Jung first spoke to me of the prophecy, when I was at
Küsnacht with Jerome in 1953, I showed him a color photograph
reproduced in *Life* magazine of the life-cell division, and I asked
if it wasn't like the saying of Maria.

"Yes," he answered, "only the reverse. I have often watched
these cells under a microscope and thought how natural it was.
This is the movement into life, and the other, the Axioma Maria,
is the same movement out of life. The necessity of the 'ten thousand things' unifying themselves, that is, the Four that is One
becomes the Three, the Three becomes the Two, the Two gives
birth to the One. You see," he added, "in the middle of a person's
life, when the birth process is finished, the reverse must begin to
take place. And here we can have some control."

No wonder it is called an enigmatic text! What does it mean?
"One becomes two, two becomes three, and out of the third
comes the one as the fourth."

Several associations came to me with the aid of Hermes, I am
sure. First, I had a feeling of growth—of expansion—like a seed
that sends forth its roots, branches, and flowers, and then I had
the feeling of a reversal of the growth, of the growth going back
into itself like a snail vanishing within its shell.

I remembered a toy that I loved to play with as a child, a
Chinese toy that was beautiful in form and texture. It was an
egg—a wooden egg, large, smooth, and lovely. One day I discov-
ered that the egg opened in half and within it lay another egg.
"From the One comes Two." Within the second egg lay a third.
"From the Two comes Three." Inside the third egg was the last

egg, the fourth, and it was painted bright red, a vermilion red. "From the Third comes the One as the Fourth."

I was enchanted with that toy; for from the four eggs I could make three, and from the three, two, and from the two, one. "The One that is Four." And then I could reverse the process. I am reminded of a poem by Lao Tzu:

> The Way begets one;
> One begets two;
> Two begets three;
> Three begets the myriad creatures.[3]

Again I think of the creation myths and of the One that emanated from the invisible, from the nothingness that was named the Primal Waters, Chaos, the Void, or the womb of nature. Out of nothingness proceeded One, the Cosmic Egg, an entity so abstract that it was considered beyond the comprehension of man. It was the source of life, complete within itself, and yet manifest. From it there emanated a great abstract cosmic pattern—a creative extension into time and space. That One could be symbolized by a circle of infinity similar to the inner circle of the Stone. Within this circle neither time nor space existed; it was a circle of emptiness that revolved within itself. The Pythagorean Greeks called it the Monad; the Chinese, T'ai Chi or the First Cause; the Zen Buddhists called it Sho, the Absolute.

Within this One a change took place, and the One became Two—dual, like the two circles of the Stone, and yet the two were thought of as one. The Greeks regarded this Two, the Duad, as the "Cosmic Mother principle, the source of all created life." The One symbolized the Sun and the Father principle, and was identified with fire and spirit. The Two symbolized the moon and the Mother principle, and was identified with water and the unconscious.

Likewise, within the primal Monad of the Chinese, the T'ai Chi, a change took place. It moved and produced Yang and Yin, the male and female principles. Though they were two, they were considered to be one; and, as with the Greeks, the male principle existed within the female and the female principle within the male. We can see this clearly in the symbol of the Great Monad, the black seed of the female lying within the male, and the white seed of the male lying within the female.

Again I think of my childhood egg, the egg that became two, and then three. On the Stone I see the sun, which stands for the One and also the Father principle. I also see the moon, which symbolizes the Two and the Mother principle. And the Child is their son, the number Three, the One that is three.

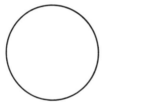

Again I notice the fire and water triangles on the Stone and the Child between the Two. The two triangles symbolize the marriage of fire and water which again produces a third: the Father, Mother, and—Son.

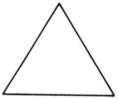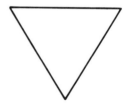

Next I see a triangle with equal sides, which has always been a mystical and spiritual symbol. It reminds me of pyramids and high mountain peaks, symbolic of aspiration and the abodes of the gods. The Greeks considered the triangle to be the most perfect geometric figure; to them it symbolized wisdom. Indeed, it is three in one and one that is three. Also, I have noticed that Hermes' cap is pyramidical in form; in Arcadia, a three-headed Mercury was worshipped. In Christianity, the triangle symbolizes the three sides of God—the Father, Son, and Holy Ghost.

Allowing my mind to wander, I think of the three primary colors, and of the three basic geometric forms: sphere, triangle, and square, all of which appear on the Stone. Furthermore, time is divided into three divisions: the past, the present, and the future. "[In] modern physics . . . according to Professor Matthews of London University, the view is gaining ground that 'the fundamental pattern of matter is itself a triangle, representing just three basic particles.'"⁴

In mythology there were usually three world divisions. And then there are the three days that Christ spent in the underworld from which he arose; the three days in the accounts of the mystery initiations and the mystic initiations and the mystic death from which rebirth took place. With the Buddhists everywhere, "The three precious things are Buddha, the law, and the assembly. . . . The images of Buddha are only represented in three positions, viz., sitting cross-legged, as if preparing to advance, and reclining on his side. . . ."⁵ Cosmic Trinities have existed from earliest times, to the present Christian Trinity, and they all are seen as symbolic of the original Cosmic Trinity, the Three in One, and the One that is Three.

The egg pattern of my equilateral triangle next becomes the Four. "From the One comes Two, from the Two, Three, and from the Third comes the One as the Fourth."

As I looked at the triangular design of the eggs, that had now become four, it gave me a feeling of expansion and descent similar to the design of the Tetractys, and reminded me again of the cosmic creation myth. From the One, the Great One beyond space and time, came an act of creation and an expansion and manifestation through limitless space. This mysterious One who held within himself the will to create, became Two, the God and the Goddess. The Two then became Three, the first active procreative energy, the Cosmic Son. The Three then became Four, the creation of form into space, the earthly son.

The four radiating lines on the Stone seem to flow out from a central source toward the four corners of the world square. Jung compared these lines to the saying of Maria Prophetissa. He also said that he ". . . found the quaternity to be the archetypal foundation of the human psyche."⁶ This same pattern is found all over the world. Four sacred streams in four directions poured out from the roots of the Buddha's four-limbed Bo tree of life. And in the Garden of Eden there were four rivers. For the Taoists and Confucianists and the Navaho Indians, there were also the four sacred mountains of the four directions. And the Mayan Indians had four direction gods called Bacabs who also supported the corners of the Mayan heaven.

There were four main Chinese characters, four root numbers, four winds, the four evangelists, the four-headed Hermes, and the four faces of Brahma. Also I must not forget the four humors—phlegmatic, sanguine, choleric, and melancholy.

The alchemist observed that the matter in his retort divided into four, the four elements, which on the Stone are symbolized by the four planetary signs: Mars (iron), Venus (copper), Jupiter (tin), and Saturn (lead). The alchemists also had four main steps in their work. An analogous correspondence seems to be the four main steps in Jung's individuation process and his four functions of consciousness: thinking, feeling, intuition, and sensation.

Dr. Jacobi says:

> The separation of the One into the Four is a process of differentiation which enhances the powers of the One and enables it to extend to all four horizons. In the sphere of psychic development a similar pattern underlies the stabilization, broadening, and maturation of the ego, which is accompanied by the progressive differentiation of the four functions of consciousness. . . .[7]

I found that if I looked upon the square on the Stone and the four radiating lines, I could see that this configuration might symbolize the breaking down of the original unity into four. Comparing this to man, it reminded me of man crucified in space, torn in different directions, man lacking in inner unity, man who longs for wholeness, for oneness.

Looking at the square and the four lines in another way, I saw Hermes' position on the Stone as an apex of a pyramid made by the four zig-zag lines—the four sides of the pyramid united by Hermes, the One that is Four. And if I then took the main construction lines of the mandala, I thought they would say to me, "Here is man liberated from identification with his four functions and therefore from the tension of opposites—man, whole within himself, which is shown by the Child in the circle, from which radiates the four-armed cross in which the opposites are at rest."

Returning to the saying of Maria the Prophetissa, "Out of the Third comes the One, as the Fourth," I take the meaning to be that out of the Three, the creative energy, comes the creation itself in the form of the Four, the One manifesting in his own creation. "Jung sees the number four," states Dr. Jacobi, "as an archetype of extraordinary significance for the psyche. With this fourth term the pure spirit received its 'bodyliness' and therefore a form of manifestation adequate to the physical creation."[8]

To me this One, manifesting in his own creation, the One that is Four, is the spirit of God buried within man, like the fire of God buried in the earth or the world-soul buried in matter. If man is a miniature cosmos, a mirror reflection of the great cosmos, then man's pattern is an image of the cosmic pattern. That would mean that in order to find this buried spirit of God within man, we must reverse the cosmic pattern and descend within ourselves, into our inner world, to find what is buried there. It is similar to what Jung did when he worked the "Uncarved Block," his Stone. But as we descend, we must relate this descending pattern to the ascending one. Transformation, the transforming steps of the four eggs into one, can take place only if we experience consciously each descending step of man's earthly pattern as also being a step upward into the heavenly one.

If we could experience these steps and finally achieve the One, would we not be standing in the center of our own circle of wholeness, like the child on the Stone? Interpreted thusly, the saying of Maria Prophetissa tells us a process, a way, not only to the secret of the Philosophers' Stone, but also to unity, that oneness within ourselves which is the "Self."

I thought I could find these two patterns on the Stone. The One could be the small inner circle, the circle of emptiness; the Two, the Sun and Moon, which are two but also one; the Three, the Child as the son, and also the Sun, Moon, and Child, a trinity which is One; the four, the large circle with the four radiating lines, and also Mercury-Hermes as the Special Child, the One that is Four.

The reverse dynamic, or man's earthly pattern of individuation, would comprise: the Four, the four antagonistic elements, or the crossed lines; the Three, the lower trinity, or the chthonic aspect of Mercury-Hermes; the Two, the positive and negative, Sun and Moon; One, Mercury-Hermes, who unites the positive and negative within himself and becomes the Self, the child Mercury-Hermes in the center of the mandala. Actually, Mercury-Hermes is symbolic of all four steps: the One that is Two, the Two that is Three, and the One that is Four. It came to me that the great cosmic pattern symbolized by the One, Two, Three, and Four—which added together are Ten, the number of completion—reveals to me that all life, even the smallest thing, proceeds from the One and returns to the One, and at the same time they are One.

The One also constitutes the river, of which Jung said: "The One had a double meaning—that's the one here on the river." This river which flows out from a central source into the four corners of the earth and into the Ocean of Life never ends. Its waters are drawn up into the heavens and purified to descend again, completing its cycle as it returns to the original source.

CHAPTER
XI

The House

The symbolism of numbers has always fascinated me. Maybe that is why numbers speak to me through my dreams, and why Hermes, in his final days with me as my guide, spoke to me only of numbers. At Küsnacht I had asked Jung what he felt about numbers, and he had said, "Yes, numbers! Numbers have always existed, within and without. Maybe they existed before the world was created. Many people have questioned whether numbers were invented or discovered. They were, of course, discovered. America was not invented; it was discovered. It has been there all along. You know, fantasy is always in the act of becoming fact. Fantasy remains fantasy until man needs it and then he makes it fact. He won't believe it until it is fact." In one of his books, speaking of numbers, Jung suggests that they "may well be the most primitive element of order in the human mind. . . . That numbers have an archetypal foundation is not, by the way, a conjecture of mine but of certain mathematicians. . . . Hence it is not such an audacious conclusion after all if we define number psychologically as an *archetype of order* which has become conscious."[1]

Marie-Louise von Franz says:

> Among the many mathematical primary intuitions, or *a priori* ideas, the "natural numbers" seem psychologically the most interesting. Not only do they serve our conscious everyday measuring and counting operations; they have for centuries been the only existing means for "reading" the meaning of such ancient forms of divination as astrology, numerology, geomancy,

etc.—all of which are based on arithmetical computation and all of which have been investigated by Jung in terms of his theory of synchronicity. Furthermore, the natural numbers— viewed from a psychological angle—must certainly be archetypal representations, for we are forced to think about them in certain definite ways. . . . But the natural numbers are also qualities adherent to outer objects: . . . Yet these same numbers are also just as indisputably parts of our own mental set-up— abstract concepts that we can study without looking at outer objects. Numbers thus appear to be a tangible connection between the spheres of matter and psyche. According to hints dropped by Jung, it is here that the most fruitful field of further investigation might be found.[2]

Speaking to Hermes in what was to be our final conversation, I said to him: "As I look at your Stone, I see that I can compare many of Jung's carvings to the symbolism of numbers. On one side of you, the side toward which you point, is the Sun, which has always been known as one, and Jupiter, three. On the other side is Venus, who is six, and the Moon, two. Above you is Saturn as eight. Beneath you is Mars as nine, and you yourself, as the planet Mercury, are five. All of you together add up to thirty-four, which I have always thought of as a very important number, since it is composed of three and four which added together equal seven, 'The Sacred Seven of the Heavenly Bodies.'"

I paused, to hear what he would say, and after a moment of silence he answered: "Yes, so now you know that I can symbolize one, two, three, and four, and five and more numbers if you are open to it."

"Well then, let me see," I said, "five is not only your number. When I was a teenager I adopted it as my own, my personal symbol, in the form of a five-pointed star. When I used it, I always made sure that the one point of the star was up, for two points up symbolize black magic and the horns of a witch. This star with the one point up also is a symbol of initiation and physical Man. He is often pictured with outstretched arms and legs, as in Leonardo's drawing. Man, the microcosm, crucified in space, the macrocosm. Five also symbolizes the *hieros gamos*, since it represents the bringing together of three, or heaven, with the two of Earth Mother. And you, Hermes the Mediator, are five, as well as four, the center point of the squared circle." There was a drawing of the five-pointed star in the entrance hall of Jung's house at Bollingen about which Jung had said: "This five-pointed star is female and negative." But I did not dare ask what it symbolized when it was reversed, for I knew it could also symbolize the positive female.

"So from the number five, and four," I said to Hermes, "we go to six. On the Stone you stand at the point of the connecting triangles of fire and water. The Greeks thought of this juncture as symbolic of the hermaphrodite."

Six was also made up of two similar interlacing triangles which stood for spirit and matter, and these in turn symbolize the higher and lower trinities, as well as the human soul.

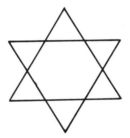

In the Hebrew tradition this hexagram is called the Star of David and Solomon's seal, and symbolizes marriage or the union of the opposites. Furthermore, six is the number of Venus; not only do we find her on the Stone, but we also find the number six, the six stones that make up part of the Stone's foundation.

When I had questioned Jung about the symbolism of the foundation, he said, "The whole base was constructed on the bases of six and two. Six had the implication of Venus—the feminine—her number. It also represented the Star of David. The Stone's foundation had three levels: the first level of six rocks; on top of them two rocks; and surmounting them the Stone as One itself."

So there are nine stones in all, eight in the foundation. Nine is Mars' number; since he was the lover of Venus, this could again symbolize the *hieros gamos*, the union of the opposites—in alchemy the "conjunction."

I pressed on to consider the meanings of the number seven. In rites of initiation, there were often seven tests to be gone through in the Underworld. These were commonly symbolized by seven steps, the seven rungs of a ladder, seven *chakras* of the Kundalini, the seven steps in the alchemists' work, and so on. The great Sumerian Goddess Inanna passed through seven gates on her way to the Underworld, and Sophia, the Goddess of Light and Wisdom, arose through seven planetary spheres. It is said that Buddha took seven steps at his birth, "Seven steps towards each of the four cardinal points."[3] And when he was about to attain *Nirvana*, he left his footprints on a carved stone; within these footprints were the Buddhist symbols known as the Seven Appearances.[4]

Speaking of Mercury, Jung says, that the seven planets are the seven metals contained in Mercury, for he is the father of metals. "When personified, he is the unity of the seven planets, an Anthropos whose body is the world. . . ."[5] He also says, "The idea of an ascent through the seven spheres of the planets symbolizes the return of the soul to the sun-god from whom it originated. . . ."[6]

In the Bible, it is recorded that the world was created in seven days. The moon changes her form every seven days. In fact, seven has always been considered a holy number. In the sacred ceremonies of India and Greece, the seven-stringed vina and the seven-stringed lyre were used; they corresponded to harmony amongst the Seven Heavenly Bodies. The seven stars of the Great Bear and the Pleiades played an important part in the religion of the American Indian. I have seen these stars on many artifacts and in the equipment of shamans.

"You have not yet mentioned, or thought of, two very important sevens," Hermes said to me. "One is actually part of me," he went on. "The other is an important object from Chaldean times, shaped like the Stone."

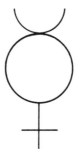

I shut my eyes and meditated on my memory of his form. "Why, yes! Why, yes! the most obvious: The sign on your body!" I said. "Your sign! The top of your sign is the crescent moon, the circle represents the sun, and the cross, the earth. Here they can symbolize the negative, positive, and formative, and combined they are solar, lunar, and hermaphroditic, and they symbolize quicksilver. Moreover, in the symbolism of numbers the moon is two, the sun is one, and the earth four—their sum equals seven.

"And as for the object shaped like the Stone," I said, the number seven having wakened a sudden thought, "there are those six-sided cubes, the dice. How could I have forgotten dice, especially since you are the god of Chance. Each side of the dice plus its opposite side, adds up to seven—seven come eleven, the magic throw."

There was something else I had not noticed earlier. "Hermes," I said, "you are in the center of a great big figure eight." Eight symbolizes balance, evolution, and regeneration. The eight resembles an hourglass, symbolizing time. It is also a symbol of Saturn. I picture the lower globe as dark and watery, the upper as light and fiery. And as I gaze on the eight, the upper, light half is beginning to dribble down drop by drop into the dark lower part. I now see the whole hourglass turn over, and the dark globe begins to drip into the lower one, now light. The spiral line of the figure eight seems to move up and down and in and out like the movement of psychic energy, reminding me of yin and yang. I can also see Hermes, lamp in hand, flying down from above into the Underworld, leading the aspirant through the dark waters and the seven tests he must pass before he can arise again into the light of consciousness and back into the creative source from which he once emerged. This creative source would be the One, or the inner circle on the Stone, which is also the eight.

In Egypt there were eight original gods, the Ogdoads. This beginning from the One, and return into the Eight which was One, is described in an Egyptian coffin text as, "I am the One who became Two. I am the Two who became Four, I am the Four who became Eight. I am the One who protects himself. I am Khepri, the Becoming One, in the Palace of the Obelisk. . . ."

Jung says of Mercury, "His dual nature enabled him to be not only the seventh but also the eighth—the eighth on Olympus 'whom nobody thought of.' "[7] In China there were the Eight Immortals of the Taoists and eight paths to Nirvana. In music, the musical octave of eight notes where the last note is the beginning of a new cycle. From a Christian Gnostic point of view, "the number eight is the symbol of rebirth through baptism, and . . . of the eternal life that finds its mystical beginning in the water and its fulfillment in the bliss and eternal peace of the divine vision."[8]

There is still another eight on the Stone, I now see, which rather resembles the eight spokes of a wheel; it reminds me of the wheel of Buddha that had eight spokes. The spokes in the wheel of the Stone are the four radiating lines and the vertical and horizontal lines of the planets. These resemble the design of the eight trigrams in the Book of Changes, *I Ching*; that ancient Oriental design symbolizes the universe and was named the Sequence of Earlier Heaven, or Primal Arrangement.[9] Like the symbols of the Stone, these eight trigrams represented four pairs of ". . . irreconcilable opposites in the phenomenal world. In the primal relationships, however, they balance each other."[10]

There are also two movements, forward expansion and backward contraction when the trigrams intermingle. The dynamic process of individuation comprises all this, as does making conscious the contents of the unconscious. Jung says of this work, ". . . [t]he *I Ching* is a formidable psychological system that endeavors to organize the play of archetypes, the 'wondrous operations of nature,' into a certain pattern, so that a 'reading' becomes possible."[11] That is exactly what Hermes and the Stone were doing for me.

I had now two more numbers to consider to complete the decade. Nine is a mysterious number, probably because it never changes. It is the treble of the sacred number three. I can multiply or add the three threes, and the sum always comes to nine. Jung's Stone is the ninth, standing on its foundation of eight stones. All numbers are contained in nine, to be reborn into a new cycle of manifestation. Maybe that is why it symbolizes initiation. It has its dark side, as everything has, and this was thought to be black magic. In the Eleusinian mysteries, initiation took place the last nine days. It takes nine months for the development of a babe in its mother's womb, and as Hindus see it, the ninth *avatar*, or embodiment of Vishnu, was Buddha. In Greece nine was consecrated to the Muses and to the "music of the spheres." The Pythagoreans described nine as flowing like the ocean around the other numbers within the decade.

And finally, coming to ten, I spoke to my guide with a certain sense of accomplishment. "Ten," I said, "is the number of perfection and completion, completion of the One, now plus its circle. You, yourself, could be One standing in your circle—together ten."

I paused to listen to his comment, but since he made none, I sought to picture him in his circle on the Stone. Was he growing smaller and smaller? He was! The Stone's large circle darkened and the crossed lines seemed to point inward and downward as Hermes sank in his circle, like a rock into the ocean. My eyes followed his descent, down, down into a dark well-circle, and way down at the bottom I saw him slowly vanish into the depth of the well. Did I see him wave goodbye to me as the waters closed over him?

Though I felt a deep pang and great sense of loss at our parting, I knew within myself that Hermes could no longer be my guide. In the role of guide he had taken on many forms, and as the creative animus had given meaning to my search, my arduous attempt not only to solve the Stone's riddles, but also to understand what the Stone's messages held for me. In our many talks, he had shed light not only on the Stone's clues but also on himself. He had become a true Opener of the Door, taking the place of Jung and Dr. L. Over a period of years, he had unmasked himself and allowed me to see and comprehend his countless forms. During this process, the spell that he had cast upon me from the very beginning had slowly evaporated. Had he not allowed this to happen, he would have become extremely dangerous, cutting me off from that very portion of myself that he was helping me to realize and assimilate; binding me to himself, the Stone, and an interest merely in symbolic forms in and for themselves. In mythic terms, he would have possessed me and carried me off. I wonder to where?

Closing my eyes, I made a wish that I should not lose *all* contact with Hermes. As if in answer, I saw a flash of light and on its ray a glimpse of Hermes-Mercury in his winged aspect flying by, caduceus in hand. In that aspect did he perhaps symbolize my intuition?

I do not doubt that the Stone is Hermes-Mercury, and Hermes-Mercury is the Stone—the Spirit of the Stone. As the element that can transform the material into the spiritual and the highest to the lowest, he is symbolic of both the alchemists' opus and the individuation process, the steps common to both processes. As the Self, Hermes-Mercury "is the mirror-image of the mystical experience . . . he represents at once the Self and the individuation process and because of the limitless number of his designations, also the collective unconscious."[12]

Looking at the mandala on the Stone, I now feel as I did in the beginning, but am graced with a new conviction: harmony and order do exist. I know that the four elements have come together, all four functions are in play, and that the squaring of the circle has been miraculously completed. The mandala shows that the individual to whom it belongs has synthesized the unconscious sides of his personality. He stands between heaven and earth; rebirth has taken place, rebirth in the new center of his psyche, which is far greater than the conscious ego, for it is the true center of man. Out of the Four he has awakened to the One —the Self. He is whole within himself.

Jung wrote in his autobiography:

> When the stone was finished, I looked at it again and again, wondering about it and asking myself what lay behind my impulse to carve it.

> The stone stands outside the Tower, and is like an explanation

of it. It is a manifestation of the occupant, but one which remains incomprehensible to others. Do you know what I wanted to chisel into the back face of the stone? *"Le cri de Merlin."* For what the stone expressed reminded me of Merlin's life in the forest, after he had vanished from the world. Men still hear his cries, so the legend runs, but they cannot understand or interpret them.

Merlin represents an attempt by the medieval unconscious to create a parallel figure to Parsifal. Parsifal is a Christian hero, and Merlin, son of the devil and a pure virgin, is his dark brother. In the twelfth century, when the legend arose, there were as yet no premises by which his intrinsic meaning could be understood. Hence he ended in exile, and hence *"le cri de Merlin"* which still sounded from the forest after his death. This cry that no one could understand implies that he lives on in unredeemed form. His story is not yet finished, and he still walks abroad. It might be said that the secret of Merlin was carried on by alchemy, primarily in the figure of Mercurius. Then Merlin was taken up again in my psychology of the unconscious and—remains uncomprehended to this day! That is because most people find it quite beyond them to live on close terms with the unconscious. Again and again I have had to learn how hard this is for people.[13]

As to that third side of the Stone that faces the lake, Jung said, "I let the stone itself speak, as it were, in a Latin inscription."[14] It reads:

"I am an orphan, alone; nevertheless I am found everywhere. I am one, but opposed to myself. I am youth and old man at one and the same time. I have known neither father nor mother, because I have had to be fetched out of the deep like a fish, or fell like a white stone from heaven. In woods and mountains I roam, but I am hidden in the innermost soul of man. I am mortal for everyone, yet I am not touched by the cycle of aeons." The first sentence is a fragment from Heraclitus; the second sentence alludes to the Mithras liturgy, and the last sentence to Homer.[15]

So the Spirit of the Stone speaks and describes himself. Might he also be describing Jung?

A few weeks before Jung died, he dreamed that he had seen a great white stone. At the bottom of the stone was the inscription: "Take this as a sign of wholeness." Jung also said: "The union of opposites in the stone is possible only when the adept has become One himself. The unity of the stone is the equivalent of individuation, by which man is made one; we would say that the stone is a projection of the unified self . . . the stone is a *transcendent* unity."[16]

It is most significant that on Jung's Stone there is one uncarved face. He must have had an important reason to leave that face of emptiness—perhaps to allow things to happen. Meditating on this thought, I closed my eyes and again clearly saw the mandala face of the Stone. I saw it in a new light, for all the small details and even the square had vanished, and only the circle with its center point stood out clearly and strongly. It even seemed to be alive. Hermes-Mercury had vanished, but his doorway, the center point, remained invitingly open.

Why, I thought, the Stone is Mercury's house, but also my psyche! And when the child Mercury-Hermes asked me to step inside his doorway, I moved into an unknown, mysterious world —the seemingly blank side of the Stone, the opposite of the mandala side. On that unknown empty space, while I searched for the Stone's treasure, I experienced my own house. For me, the house symbolizes my own psyche. Within it there is the possibility of a transformation.

During my long analysis I had had many dreams of houses. Maybe those would now tell me the story of my own personal myth in search of the treasure, and let me know in what house my true treasure lies.

What does a house symbolize to me? As I ponder that question, I first picture a natural shelter like a cave. Then I see brush shelters or animal-skin tents, which eventually develop into abodes made of rocks, clay, or wood. These take the forms of dwellings of sacred temples. Furthermore, the house is closely connected with the mother and the mysteries of the feminine and transformation. For me, the house must symbolize my own psyche, in which there is the possibility of a transformation similar to that in the vase dream I had at the commencement of my transference.

The following dreams, which I experienced with the help of Jung, Dr. L., and Hermes, will relate my myth:

Shortly after I began my analysis I had a dream in which I declared I was going to build my own house and its construction must be Chinese. So it was not strange to me when many of my dreams took place thereafter in China, Japan, or Tibet. I associate these lands with the Wisdom of the Way, the Tao.

After five years of analysis I dreamt that a house burned to the ground, and two years later I had a dream in which my own house burned, leaving only an outer shell.

After that, in another dream, I moved into my own house, a one-room stone house in Tibet which contained all that I needed.

In reality I lived in a house that I had bought at Big Sur that was too large for me. I named it Big Star Way after a Navaho ceremony. I decided now to build a smaller house—*my house*. Nature provided the material for its main wall, which was made up of stones found on the highway after storms. With the help of a neighbor-friend, I designed a house, the kind I had always wanted, influenced by the Japanese. It gave the feeling that when one stepped inside the door, nature also entered—a marriage between the natural surroundings and the house itself. Within a year or more, I moved into the new house, taking with me the books and files I needed for my present work and some of the objects I was fond of. I named the new house "Little Star Way." Friends rented my old house.

Several months later an almost apocalyptic event occurred. It was noon, and I was lying on the sofa on my back after eating an early lunch. First my poodle barked, seemingly at nothing. Then I heard a strange crackling noise that seemed to come from outside. When I opened the front door to investigate, and looked up in the direction of the noise, I was horrified to see flames and billowing smoke shooting out of the kitchen end of the old big house. Realizing that I myself could do little about it, I rushed inside and telephoned the Big Sur Forest Service. They told me it would take thirty-five minutes for their fire truck to reach me. I then telephoned every man on the ridge for help. Not one answered; they were all away.

As a last resort, I ran to my next-door neighbor's house and found her lying on a chaise longue in a lace negligée. In a high, excited voice I asked her to go for help immediately—male help

—as my house was burning down. She went off in her car in her negligée. I did not call my friend Louisa, since I knew she had a badly sprained ankle.

I climbed the hill toward the raging fire, pulling the hose behind me, and found the whole house was in flames. I tried to open the studio door to rescue my work, but the flames stopped me. My next-door neighbor arrived, but without any male help. Then I thought of turning off the electricity and gas switches, which were on the outside of the house. Next to them I found a can of gasoline and kerosene and moved them to safety.

Hearing a voice, I turned around and there was Louisa hobbling along. She had run all the way on her injured ankle. Such are friends at Big Sur. We attached more hoses, but it did little good. My fear was that the fire might spread to my neighbors' houses.

The fire truck at last arrived. We were so exhausted from the intense heat and flames, the smoke, and our inability to accomplish anything, that we hardly realized that we had help—man-made help. By four o'clock, the fire was out and the house was reduced to ashes, blackened bricks, and charred wood.

As Louisa and I descended the hill, leaving behind the remains of what had been, my thoughts suddenly took over as we entered "Little Star Way." What a shock to realize that I had lost everything—all my past work, my unique library, paintings, and family antiques. Though it was a warm day, I shuddered with chills. Louisa told me I was in shock. With the aid of a scotch and soda, I began to relax, and a very comforting thought came to me. I remembered a previous dream that I suddenly understood.

> *I was in an apartment in New York City by the East River. At dusk I went for a walk and at a great distance I saw a huge orb sinking. On its surface were crossed lines similar to Jung's Stone. I said to myself: Why, those are the pathways on the moon. To the left of the sinking sun I saw a much smaller orb rising and said: Why, this is the moon; the larger one, the sun.*

This dream told me that the rising moon symbolized the new birth of my real feminine nature into consciousness. So I looked on the burning of my old house and its contents as a necessary destruction of my past life. The new house became the outer

manifestation of my inner work—my new life. It was at this time
that Alan Watts blessed the new house in a pagan ceremony.
Later I dreamt:

> *I went to the house of a Zen Priest that I knew in real life. He*
> *was seated on the floor with his followers about him. I sat in*
> *front of him and he gave me a present of a small box. I opened*
> *it and found within a small figure in lotus position and I thought*
> *it must be the Buddha. Underneath the box and yet a part of it*
> *were three tiny drawers which I opened and found within silks of*
> *all colors. A woman friend (a shadow figure) threw herself down*
> *in front of the priest in a most undignified manner, which I did*
> *not like. She left and again I sat in front of him and opened the*
> *box again. Within I saw the Buddha seated on a tiny throne. I*
> *said: "It is the Buddha on a throne," and the priest said, "Yes."*

I knew this was a wonderful dream—the God within. Yet
something warned me not to get too excited or inflated. Also I
thought of the other woman figure as my own negative shadow
side, to be observed and understood, and of the Zen religion
which spoke to me much more than any western religion. Yet, I
did not want to be a part of any organized religious group. I
must find for myself the God within that lies between East and
West, between Buddha and Christ. The Zen priest was in the role
of a spiritual animus. In real life he was an extraordinary man
and a great influence on me. I knew he understood the lonely
journey on my Path.

Notes

Chapter II   The Beginning

1. C. G. Jung, *Memories, Dreams, Reflections* (New York: Random House, 1961), p. 227, note 2. "The first sentence is a fragment from Heraclitus; the second sentence alludes to the Mithras liturgy, and the last sentence to Homer."

2. *Ibid.*, p. 227.

3. *Ibid.*, pp. 225–26.

4. *Cf.* C. G. Jung, "Flying Saucers: A Modern Myth of Things Seen in the Skies," in *The Collected Works of C. G. Jung*, trans. R. F. C. Hull, Bollingen Series XX, Vol. 10, *Civilization in Transition* (Princeton: Princeton University Press, 1964, 1970) pp. 307–433 [hereinafter cited as *Collected Works*].

Chapter III   Stones

1. T. S. Eliot, from "Four Quartets, Little Gidding," in *Collected Poems, 1909–1962* (London: Faber and Faber Ltd. 1963), pp. 221–22.

2. Joseph Campbell, Jeff King, and Maud Oakes, *Where the Two Came to Their Father*, Bollingen Series I (New York: Pantheon Books, 1943).

3. C. G. Jung, "Approaching the Unconscious," in *Man and His Symbols* (Garden City, N.Y.: Doubleday & Co., 1964), p. 23.

4. Holmes Welch, *Taoism: The Parting of the Way* (Boston: Beacon Press, 1966), p. 40.

5. C. G. Jung in *Collected Works*, Vol. 10, *Civilization in Transition* (Princeton: Princeton University Press, 1964, 1970), par 304.

6. Arthur Waley, *The Way and Its Power* (Boston and New York: Houghton Mifflin Company, 1935), p. 58.

7. John Wier Perry, *The Self in Psychotic Process.*

8. C. G. Jung, "Approaching the Unconscious," in *Man and His Symbols* (Garden City, N.Y.: Doubleday & Co., 1964), p. 23.

9. C. G. Jung, *Memories, Dreams, Reflections* (New York: Random House, 1961), p. 399.

10. Arthur Waley, *The Way and Its Power* (Boston and New York: Houghton Mifflin and Company, 1935), p. 146.

11. T. S. Eliot, from "Four Quartets, East Coker," in *Collected Poems, 1909–1962* (London: Faber and Faber Ltd., 1963), p. 201.

12. Miguel Serrano, *C. G. Jung and Hermann Hesse* (New York: Schocken Books, 1966).

Chapter IV   The Search

1. Dr. Szent-Gyorgi, *Scope Weekly*, June 5, 1957.

2. Arthur Waley, *The Way and Its Power* (Boston and New York: Houghton Mifflin Company, 1935), p. 56.

3. C. G. Jung, "Approaching the Unconscious," in *Man and His Symbols* (Garden City, N.Y.: Doubleday & Co., 1964), pp. 98–99.

4. *Ibid.*, p. 69.

5. C. G. Jung, *Memories, Dreams, Reflections* (New York: Random House, 1961), p. 208.

6. *Ibid.*, p. 346.

7. Arthur Waley, *The Way and Its Power* (Boston and New York: Houghton Mifflin Company, 1935), p. 112.

8. Lin Yutang, *The Wisdom of China and India* (New York: Modern Library, 1942), p. 584.

9. C. G. Jung, *Psychological Reflections: An Anthology*, J. Jacobi and R. F. C. Hull, eds., Bollingen Series XXXI (Princeton: Princeton University Press, 1953, 1970), p. 29.

10. Jolande Jacobi, *The Way of Individuation* (New York: Harcourt Brace Jovanovich, 1965), p. 35.

Chapter V   Creation

1. *Popol Vuh* (Quche, Mayan Indian), Andres Recinos, tr. (publisher and date unknown), p. 81.

2. Jolande Jacobi, *The Way of Individuation* (New York: Harcourt Brace Jovanovich, 1965), pp. 64–65. Emphasis added.

3. Arthur Waley, *The Way and Its Power* (Boston and New York: Houghton Mifflin Company, 1935), p. 174.

4. Erich Neumann, "Die Angst vor dem Weiblichen," in *Die Angst*, Studies of the C. G. Jung Institute/Zurich, Vol. X (Zurich: Rascher Verlag, 1959).

Chapter VI   The Unknown World

1. C. G. Jung, "Approaching the Unconscious," in *Man and His Symbols* (Garden City, N.Y.: Doubleday & Company, 1964), p. 28.

2. Alan McGlashan, *The Savage and Beautiful Country* (Boston: Houghton Mifflin Co., 1967), p. 135.

3. Erich Neumann, *The Great Mother*, R. Manheim, trans., Bollingen Series XLVII (Princeton: Princeton University Press, 1955), p. 283.

4. Arthur Waley, *The Way and Its Power* (Boston and New York: Houghton Mifflin Company, 1935), p. 155.

5. C. G. Jung, "The Practice of Psychotherapy," in *Collected Works*, Vol. 16 (Princeton: Princeton University Press, 1966), pars. 283, 284.

6. Erich Neumann, *Amor and Psyche: The Psychic Development of the Feminine*, trans. Ralph Manheim. Bollingen Series LIV (Princeton: Princeton University Press, 1956, 1973), p. 64.

7. C. G. Jung, "The Psychology of the Transference," in *Collected Works*, Vol. 16, *The Practice of Psychotherapy* (Princeton: Princeton University Press, 1954, 1966), par. 539.

Chapter VII   The Inner Way

1. Saladin Reps and Noyogen Senzaki, *The Gateless Gate* (John Murray, date unknown), p. 8.

2. C. G. Jung, in *Collected Works*, Vol. 7, *Two Essays on Analytical Psychology* (Princeton: Princeton University Press, 1953, 1966), par. 186.

3. C. G. Jung, *Commentary on "The Secret of the Golden Flower,"* R. Wilhelm, trans. (New York: Harcourt Brace Jovanovich, 1931, 1962), p. 11.

4. Joseph Henderson, "Ancient Myths and Modern Man," in *Man and His Symbols* (Garden City, N.Y.: Doubleday & Co., 1964), pp. 132, 134.

5. T. S. Eliot, from "The Hollow Men," in *Collected Poems, 1909–1962* (London: Faber and Faber Ltd., 1963), p. 92.

6. Arthur Waley, *The Way and Its Power* (Boston and New York: Houghton Mifflin Company, 1935), p. 159.

7. C. G. Jung in *Collected Works*, Vol. 7, *Two Essays on Analytical Psychology* (Princeton: Princeton University Press, 1953, 1966), par. 331.

8. *Ibid.*, pars. 398, 399.

9. T. S. Eliot, from "Four Quartets, Burnt Norton," in *Collected Poems, 1909–1962* (London: Faber and Faber Ltd., 1963), p. 191.

Chapter VIII   A Conversation with Hermes

1. C. G. Jung, in *Collected Works*, Vol. 14, *Mysterium Coniunctionis* (Princeton: Princeton University Press, 1965, 1970), par. 289.

2. C. G. Jung and C. Kerenyi, *Essays on a Science of Mythology*, trans. R. F. C. Hull, Bollingen Series XXII (Princeton: Princeton University Press, 1949), p. 128.

3. C. G. Jung in *Collected Works*, Vol. 12, *Psychology and Alchemy* (Princeton: Princeton University Press, 1953, 1968), par. 460.

4. *Ibid.*, par. 404.

Chapter IX   The Kingdom of the Child

1. C. G. Jung, *Memories, Dreams, Reflections* (New York: Random House, 1961), p. 227.

2. Alan Watts, *Myth and Ritual in Christianity* (London and New York: Thames and Hudson, 1954), pp. 96–97, n.4.

3. Arthur Waley, *The Way and Its Power* (Boston and New York: Houghton Mifflin and Company, 1935), p. 183.

4. C. G. Jung, *Memories, Dreams, Reflections* (New York: Random House, 1961), p. 227.

5. T. S. Eliot, from "Four Quartets, Burnt Norton," in *Collected Poems, 1909–1962* (London: Faber and Faber Ltd., 1963), pp. 189, 194.

6. Marie-Louise von Franz, "Science and the Unconscious," in *Man and his Symbols* (Garden City, N.Y.: Doubleday & Co. Inc., 1964), p. 306.

7. Henrich Zimmer, *Philosophies of India*, J. Campbell, ed., Bollingen Series XXVI (New York: Pantheon Books, 1951), p. 368.

8. Rainer Maria Rilke, "The Duino Elegies," in *Selected Works*, Vol. II (Norfolk, Ct.: A New Directions Book, 1960), p. 233.

9. Jolande Jacobi, *The Psychology of C. G. Jung* (New Haven: Yale University Press, 1943, 1968), p. 80.

10. C. G. Jung, *Memories, Dreams, Reflections* (New York: Random House, 1961), p. 23.

11. C. G. Jung and C. Kerenyi, *Essays on a Science of Mythology*, trans. R. F. C. Hull. Bollingen Series XXII (Princeton: Princeton University Press, 1949), p. 130.

12. C. G. Jung, *Symbols of Transformation*, in *Collected Works*, Vol. 5 (Princeton: Princeton University Press, 1956, 1967), par. 460.

13. Mai-mai Sze, *The Tao of Painting*, Vol. I, Bollingen Series XLIX (New York: Pantheon Books, 1956), p. 28.

14. C. G. Jung, *Memories, Dreams, Reflections* (New York: Random House, 1961), pp. 353–54.

Chapter X

1. C. G. Jung, *Memories, Dreams, Reflections* (New York: Random House, 1961), pp. 205–206.
2. C. G. Jung in *Collected Works*, Vol. 12, *Psychology and Alchemy* (Princeton: Princeton University Press, 1953, 1968), par. 26.
3. Lao Tzu, *Tao Te Ching*, D. C. Lau, tr. (Baltimore, Md.: Penguin Books, 1963), p. 103.
4. Alan McGlashan, *The Savage and Beautiful Country* (Boston: Houghton Mifflin Co., 1967), p. 152.
5. C. A. S. Williams, *Outlines of Chinese Symbolism and Art Motives* (Shanghai: Kelly and Walsh, Ltd., 1941), p. 295.
6. Jolande Jacobi, *Complex/Archetype/Symbol in the Psychology of C. G. Jung*, R. Manheim, trans., Bollingen Series LVII (New York: Pantheon Books, 1959), p. 168.
7. *Ibid.*, p. 173.
8. *Ibid.*, p. 168.

Chapter XI   The House

1. C. G. Jung in *Collected Works*, Vol. 8, *The Structure and Dynamics of the Psyche* (Princeton: Princeton University Press, 1969), par. 870.
2. Marie-Louise von Franz, "Science and the Unconscious," in *Man and His Symbols* (New York: Random House, 1964), p. 310.
3. Elisabeth Goldsmith, *Life Symbols* (New York: G. P. Putnam's Sons, 1928), p. 212.
4. C. A. S. Williams, *Outlines of Chinese Symbolism and Art Motives* (Shanghai: Kelly and Walsh, Ltd., 1941), p. 194.
5. C. G. Jung in *Collected Works*, Vol. 16, *The Practice of Psychotherapy* (Princeton: Princeton University Press, 1966), par. 402.
6. C. G. Jung in *Collected Works*, Vol. 12, *Psychology and Alchemy* (Princeton: Princeton University Press, 1953, 1968), par. 66.
7. *Ibid.*, par. 84.
8. Ralph Manheim, trans., "The Mysteries," in *Papers from the Eranos Yearbooks*, Vol. 2, Bollingen Series XXX.2 (New York: Pantheon Books, 1955), p. 393. Representation of "wheel" from the Temple of the Sun in Konarak, India, as reproduced in *The Herder Symbol Dictionary*, B. Matthews, trans. (Wilmette, Ill.: Chiron Publications, 1986).
9. C. F. Baynes and Ralph Manheim, trans., *The I Ching, or Book of Changes*, Vol. 1, Bollingen Series XIX (New York: Pantheon Books, 1950), p. 285.
10. *Ibid.*, p. 286.
11. C. G. Jung in *Collected Works*, Vol. 14, *Mysterium Coniunctionis* (Princeton: Princeton University Press, 1965, 1970), par. 401.
12. C. G. Jung in *Collected Works*, Vol. 13, *Alchemical Studies* (Princeton: Princeton University Press, 1967), par. 284.
13. C. G. Jung, *Memories, Dreams, Reflections* (New York: Random House, 1961), p. 228.
14. *Ibid.*, p. 227.
15. *Ibid.*, note 2.
16. C. G. Jung in *Collected Works*, Vol. 9/ii, *Aion: Researches into the Phenomenology of the Self* (Princeton: Princeton University Press, 1959), par. 264.

Bibliography

Baynes, C. F., and R. Manheim, trans. 1950. *The I-Ching or Book of Changes*. Bollingen Series XIX. New York: Pantheon Books.

Campbell, J., J. King, and M. Oakes. 1943. *Where the Two Came to Their Father*. Bollingen Series I. New York: Pantheon Books.

Eliot, T. S. 1963. *Collected Poems, 1909–1962*. London: Faber & Faber.

Franz, M-L. von. 1964. "Science and the Unconscious." In *Man and His Symbols*. Chicago: J. G. Ferguson Publishing Company.

Goldsmith, E. 1928. *Life Symbols*. New York: G. P. Putnam's Sons.

Henderson, J. 1964. "Ancient Myths and Modern Man." In *Man and His Symbols*, C. G. Jung et al. Chicago: J. G. Ferguson Publishing Company.

Henderson, J. L., and M. Oakes. 1963. *Wisdom of the Serpent*. New York: Braziller.

Jacobi, J. 1943. *The Psychology of C. G. Jung*. New Haven: Yale University Press, 1968.

_____. 1959. *Complex/Archetype/Symbol in the Psychology of C. G. Jung*, R. Manheim, trans. Bollingen Series LVII. New York: Pantheon Books.

_____. 1965. *The Way of Individuation*. New York: Harcourt Brace Jovanovich.

Jung, C. G. 1931. *Commentary on "The Secret of the Golden Tower."* R. Wilhelm, trans. New York: Harcourt Brace Jovanovich, 1962.

_____. 1953. *Psychological Reflections: An Anthology*. J. Jacobi and R. F. C. Hull, eds. Bollingen Series XXXI. Princeton: Princeton University Press.

_____. 1953. *Psychology and Alchemy. Collected Works*, Vol. 12. Bollingen Series XX. Princeton: Princeton University Press, 1968.

_____. 1953. *Two Essays on Analytic Psychology. Collected Works*, Vol. 7. Bollingen Series XX. Princeton: Princeton University Press, 1966.

————. 1954. *Practice of Psychotherapy. Collected Works*, Vol. 16. Bollingen Series XX. Princeton: Princeton University Press, 1966.

————. 1956. *Symbols of Transformation. Collected Works*, Vol. 5. Bollingen Series XX. Princeton: Princeton University Press, 1967.

————. 1961. *Memories, Dreams, Reflections*. New York: Random House.

————. 1964. *Civilization in Transition*. R. F. C. Hull, trans. *Collected Works*, Vol. 10. Bollingen Series XX. Princeton: Princeton University Press, 1970.

———— et al. 1964. *Man and His Symbols*. Chicago: J. G. Ferguson Publishing Company.

————. 1965. *Mysterium Coniunctionis. Collected Works*, Vol. 14. Bollingen Series XX. Princeton: Princeton University Press, 1970.

————. 1967. *Alchemical Studies. Collected Works*, Vol. 13. Bollingen Series XX. Princeton: Princeton University Press.

————. 1969. *The Structure and Dynamics of the Psyche. Collected Works*, Vol. 8. Bollingen Series XX. Princeton: Princeton University Press, 1981.

————, and C. Kerenyi. 1949. *Essays on Science of Mythology*. R. F. C. Hull, trans. Bollingen Series XXII. Princeton: Princeton University Press.

Lao Tzu. 1963. *Tao Te Ching*. D. C. Lau, trans. Baltimore: Penguin Books.

Manheim, R., trans. 1955. *Papers from the Eranos Yearbooks*. Vol. 2. Bollingen Series XXX. New York: Pantheon Books.

McGlashan, A. 1967. *The Savage and Beautiful Country*. Boston: Houghton Mifflin Company.

Neumann, E. 1955. *The Great Mother*. R. Manheim, trans. Bollingen Series XLVII. Princeton: Princeton University Press.

————. 1956. *Amor and Psyche: The Psychic Development of the Feminine*. R. Manheim, trans. Bollingen Series LIV. Princeton: Princeton University Press, 1973.

————. 1959. "Die Angst vor dem Weiblichen." In *Studies of the C. G. Jung Institute*. Vol. X. Zurich: Rascher Verlag.

Oakes, M. 1951. *Beyond the Windy Place.* London: Gollancz.

_____. 1951. *Two Crosses of Todos Santos.* New York: Pantheon Books. 2nd ed. 1969. Princeton: Princeton University Press.

Perry, J. W., 1951. *The Self in Psychotic Process.* Berkeley: University of California Press.

Reps, S., and N. Senzake. *The Gateless Gate.* John Murray.

Rilke, R. M. 1960. "The Duino Elegies." In *Selected Works.* Vol. 2. Norfolk, Conn.: A New Directions Book.

Serrano, M. 1966. C. G. *Jung and Hermann Hesse.* New York: Schocken Books.

Sze, M. 1956. *The Tao of Painting.* Vol. 1. Bollingen Series XLIV. New York: Pantheon Books.

Waley, A. 1935. *The Way and Its Power.* Boston and New York: Houghton Mifflin Company.

Watts, A. 1954. *Myth and Ritual in Christianity.* London and New York: Thames and Hudson.

Welch, H. 1966. *Taoism: The Parting of the Way.* Boston: Beacon Press.

Williams, C. A. S. 1941. *Outlines of Chinese Symbolism and Art Motives.* Shanghai: Kelly and Walsh, Ltd.

Zimmer, H. 1951. *Philosophies of India.* J. Campbell, ed. Bollingen Series XXVI. New York: Pantheon Books.

Index